INTERIM REPORT OF

THE PRESIDENT'S TASK FORCE ON
21ST CENTURY POLICING

Recommended citation:

President's Task Force on 21st Century Policing. 2015. *Interim Report of the President's Task Force on 21st Century Policing*. Washington, DC: Office of Community Oriented Policing Services.

First published March 1, 2015
Revised March 4, 2015

Contents

From the Co-Chairs

We wish to thank President Barack Obama for giving us the honor and privilege of leading the Task Force on 21st Century Policing. The task force was created to strengthen community policing and trust among law enforcement officers and the communities they serve, especially in light of recent events around the country that have underscored the need for and importance of lasting collaborative relationships between local police and the public. We found engaging with law enforcement officials, technical advisors, youth and community leaders, and nongovernmental organizations through a transparent public process to be both enlightening and rewarding, and we again thank him for this honor.

Given the urgency of these issues, the President gave the task force an initial 90 days to identify best practices and offer recommendations on how policing practices can promote effective crime reduction while building public trust. In this short period, the task force conducted seven public listening sessions across the country and received testimony and recommendations from a wide range of community and faith leaders, law enforcement officers, academics, and others to ensure these recommendations would be informed by a diverse range of voices. Such a remarkable achievement could not have been accomplished without the tremendous assistance provided by the U.S. Department of Justice's Office of Community Oriented Policing Services (COPS Office), led by Director Ronald L. Davis, who also served as the executive director of the task force. We thank Director Davis for his leadership, as well as his chief of staff, Melanca Clark, and the COPS Office team that supported the operation and administration of the task force.

We also wish to extend our appreciation to the COPS Office's extremely capable logistical and technical assistance provider, Strategic Applications International (SAI), led by James and Colleen Copple. In addition to logistical support, SAI digested the voluminous information received from testifying witnesses and the public in record time and helped facilitate the task force's deliberations on recommendations for the President. We are also grateful for the thoughtful assistance of Darrel Stephens and Stephen Rickman, our technical advisors.

Most important, we would especially like to thank the hundreds of community members, law enforcement officers and executives, associations and stakeholders, researchers and academics, and civic leaders nationwide who stepped forward to support the efforts of the task force and to lend their experience and expertise during the development of the recommendations contained in this report. The passion and commitment shared by all to building strong relationships between law enforcement and communities became a continual source of inspiration and encouragement to the task force.

The dedication of our fellow task force members and their commitment to the process of arriving at consensus around these recommendations is also worth acknowledging. The task force members brought diverse perspectives to the table and were able to come together to engage in meaningful dialogue on emotionally charged issues in a respectful and effective manner. We believe the type of constructive dialogue we have engaged in should serve as example of the type of dialogue that must occur in communities throughout the nation.

While much work remains to be done to address many longstanding issues and challenges—not only within the field of law enforcement but also within the broader criminal justice system—this experience has demonstrated to us that Americans are, by nature, problem solvers. It is our hope that the recommendations included here will meaningfully contribute to our nation's efforts to increase trust between law enforcement and the communities they protect and serve.

Charles H. Ramsey
Co-Chair

Laurie O. Robinson
Co-Chair

Members of the Task Force

Co-Chairs

Charles Ramsey, Commissioner, Philadelphia Police Department

Laurie Robinson, Professor, George Mason University

Members

Cedric L. Alexander, Deputy Chief Operating Officer for Public Safety, DeKalb County, Georgia

Jose Lopez, Lead Organizer, Make the Road New York

Tracey L. Meares, Walton Hale Hamilton Professor of Law, Yale Law School

Brittany N. Packnett, Executive Director, Teach For America, St. Louis, Missouri

Susan Lee Rahr, Executive Director, Washington State Criminal Justice Training Commission

Constance Rice, Co-Director, Advancement Project

Sean Michael Smoot, Director and Chief Counsel, Police Benevolent & Protective Association of Illinois

Bryan Stevenson, Founder and Executive Director, Equal Justice Initiative

Roberto Villaseñor, Chief of Police, Tucson Police Department

Task Force Staff

The U.S. Department of Justice's Office of Community Oriented Policing Services, led by Director Ronald L. Davis, provided administrative services, funds, facilities, staff, equipment, and other support services as necessary for the task force to carry out its mission:

Executive Director	Ronald L. Davis
Chief of Staff	Melanca Clark
Communications Director	Silas Darden (Office of Justice Programs)
General Counsel	Charlotte Grzebien
External Affairs Liaison	Danielle Ouellette
External Affairs Liaison	Sheryl Thomas
Legislative Liaison	Shannon Long
Project Manager	Deborah Spence
Senior Policy Advisor	Katherine McQuay
Site Manager	Laurel Matthews
Special Assistant	Michael Franko
Special Assistant	Jennifer Rosenberger
Writer	Janice Delaney (Office of Justice Programs)
Writer	Faye Elkins

Strategic Applications International (SAI):[1] James Copple, Colleen Copple, Jessica Drake, Jason Drake, Steven Minson, Letitia Harmon, Anthony Coulson, Mike McCormack, Shawnee Bigelow, Monica Palacio, and Adrienne Semidey

Technical Advisors: Stephen Rickman and Darrel Stephens

Consultant Research Assistants: Jan Hudson, Yasemin Irvin-Erickson, Katie Jares, Erin Kearns, Belen Lowrey, and Kristina Lugo

---

[1] SAI provided technical and logistical support through a cooperative agreement with the COPS Office.

Acknowledgments

The task force received support from other components of the U.S. Department of Justice, including the Office of Justice Programs, led by Assistant Attorney General Karol Mason, and the Civil Rights Division, led by Acting Assistant Attorney General Vanita Gupta.

The following individuals from across the U.S. Department of Justice also assisted the task force in its work: Eric Agner, Amin Aminfar, Pete Brien, Pamela Cammarata, Erin Canning, Ed Chung, Caitlin Currie, Shanetta Cutlar, Melissa Fox, Shirlethia Franklin, Ann Hamilton, Najla Haywood, Esteban Hernandez, Arthur Gary, Tammie Gregg, Valerie Jordan, Mark Kappelhoff, John Kim, Kevin Lewis, Robert Listenbee, Cynthia Pappas, Scott Pestridge, Channing Phillips, Donte Turner, Melissa Randolph, Margaret Richardson, Janice Rodgers, Elizabeth Simpson, Jonathan Smith, Brandon Tramel, and Miriam Vogel.

Introduction

Trust between law enforcement agencies and the people they protect and serve is essential in a democracy. It is key to the stability of our communities, the integrity of our criminal justice system, and the safe and effective delivery of policing services.

In light of the recent events that have exposed rifts in the relationships between local police and the communities they protect and serve, on December 18, 2014, President Barack Obama signed an Executive Order establishing the Task Force on 21st Century Policing.

In establishing the task force, the President spoke of the distrust that exists between too many police departments and too many communities—the sense that in a country where our basic principle is equality under the law, too many individuals, particularly young people of color, do not feel as if they are being treated fairly.

"When any part of the American family does not feel like it is being treated fairly, that's a problem for all of us," said the President. "It's not just a problem for some. It's not just a problem for a particular community or a particular demographic. It means that we are not as strong as a country as we can be. And when applied to the criminal justice system, it means we're not as effective in fighting crime as we could be."

These remarks underpin the philosophical foundation for the Task Force on 21st Century Policing: to build trust between citizens and their peace officers so that all components of a community are treating one another fairly and justly and are invested in maintaining public safety in an atmosphere of mutual respect. Decades of research and practice tell us that the public cares as much about how police interact with them as they care about the outcomes that legal actions produce. People are more likely to obey the law when they believe those who are enforcing it have the right—the legitimate authority—to tell them what to do.[2] Building trust and legitimacy, therefore, is not just a policing issue. It involves all components of the criminal justice system and is inextricably bound to bedrock issues affecting the community such as poverty, education, and public health.

The mission of the task force was to examine how to foster strong, collaborative relationships between local law enforcement and the communities they protect and to make recommendations to the President on how policing practices can promote effective crime reduction while building public trust. The president selected members of the task force based on their ability to contribute to its mission because of their relevant perspective, experience, or subject matter expertise in policing, law enforcement and community relations, civil rights, and civil liberties.

---

[2] T.R. Tyler, *Why People Obey the Law* (New Haven, CT: Yale University Press, 1990); M.S. Frazer, *The Impact of the Community Court Model on Defendant Perceptions of Fairness: A Case Study at the Red Hook Community Justice Center* (New York: Center for Court Innovation, 2006).

The task force was given 90 days to conduct hearings, review the research, and make recommendations to the President, so its focus was sharp and necessarily limited. It concentrated on defining the cross-cutting issues affecting police-community interactions, questioning the contemporary relevance and truth about long-held assumptions about the nature and methods of policing, and identifying the areas where research is needed to highlight examples of evidence-based policing practices compatible with present realities.

To fulfill this mission, the task force convened seven listening sessions to hear testimony—including recommendations for action—from government officials; law enforcement officers; academic experts; technical advisors; leaders from established nongovernmental organizations, including grass-roots movements; and any other members of the public who wished to comment. The listening sessions were held in Washington, D.C., January 13; Cincinnati, Ohio, January 30–31; Phoenix, Arizona, February 13–14; and again in Washington, D.C., February 23–24. Other forms of outreach included a number of White House listening sessions to engage other constituencies, such as people with disabilities, the LGBTQ community, and members of the armed forces, as well as careful study of scholarly articles, research reports, and written contributions from informed experts in various fields relevant to the task force's mission.

Each of the seven public listening sessions addressed a specific aspect of policing and police-community relations, although cross-cutting issues and concerns made their appearance at every session. At the first session, **Building Trust and Legitimacy**, the topic of procedural justice was discussed as a foundational necessity in building public trust. Subject matter experts also testified as to the meaning of "community policing" in its historical and contemporary contexts, defining the difference between implicit bias and racial discrimination—two concepts at the heart of perceived difficulties between police and the people. Witnesses from community organizations stressed the need for more police involvement in community affairs as an essential component of their crime fighting duties. Police officers gave the beat cop's perspective on protecting people who do not respect their authority, and three big-city mayors told of endemic budgetary obstacles to addressing policing challenges.

The session on **Policy and Oversight** again brought witnesses from diverse police forces—both chiefs and union representatives—from law and academia and from established civil rights organizations and grass-root groups. They discussed use of force from the point of view of both research and policy and internal and external oversight; explained how they prepare for and handle mass demonstrations; and pondered culture and diversity in law enforcement. Witnesses filled the third session, on **Technology and Social Media**, with testimony on the use of body-worn cameras and other technologies from the angles of research and legal considerations, as well as the intricacies of implementing new technologies in the face of privacy issues. They discussed the ever-expanding ubiquity of social media and its power to work both for and against policing practice and public safety.

The **Community Policing and Crime Reduction** Listening Session considered current research on the effectiveness of community policing on bringing down crime, as well as building up public trust. Task force members heard detailed descriptions of the methods chiefs in cities of varying sizes used to implement effective community policing in their jurisdictions over a number of years. They also heard from a panel of young people about their encounters with the criminal justice system and the lasting effects of positive interactions with police through structured programs as well as individual relationships. The fifth listening session considered **Training and Education** in law enforcement over an officer's entire career—from recruitment through basic training to in-service training—and the support, education, and training of supervisors, leaders, and managers. Finally, the panel on **Officer Safety and Wellness** considered the spectrum of mental and physical health issues faced by police officers, from the day-to-day stress of the job, its likely effect on an officer's physical health, and the need for mental health screening, to traffic accidents, burnout, suicide, and how better to manage these issues to determine the length of an officer's career.

A Listening Session on the **Future of Community Policing** concluded the task force's public sessions and was followed by the deliberations leading to the recommendations that follow on ways to research, improve, support, and implement policies and procedures for effective policing in the 21st century.

Many excellent and specific suggestions emerged from these listening sessions on all facets of policing in the 21st century, but many questions arose as well. Paramount among them was how to bring unity of purpose and consensus on best practices to a nation with 18,000 separate law enforcement agencies and a strong history of a preference for local control of local issues. It became very clear that it is time for a comprehensive and multifaceted examination of all the interrelated parts of the criminal justice system and a focused investigation into how poverty, lack of education, mental health, and other social conditions cause or intersect with criminal behavior. We propose two overarching recommendations that will seek the answers to these questions.

0.1 OVERARCHING RECOMMENDATION: The President should support and provide funding for the creation of a National Crime and Justice Task Force to review and evaluate all components of the criminal justice system for the purpose of making recommendations to the country on comprehensive criminal justice reform.

Several witnesses at the task force's listening sessions pointed to the fact that police represent the "face" of the criminal justice system to the public. Yet police are obviously not responsible for laws or incarceration policies that many citizens find unfair. This misassociation leads us to call for a broader examination of such issues as drug policy, sentencing and incarceration, which are beyond the scope of a review of police practices.

This is not a new idea.

In the 1967 President's Commission on Law Enforcement and Administration of Justice report, *The Challenge of Crime in a Free Society*, one of the major findings stated, "Officials of the criminal justice system . . . must re-examine what they do. They must be honest about the system's shortcomings with the public and with themselves."[3]

The need to establish a formal structure to take a continuous look at criminal justice reform in the context of broad societal issues has never faded from public consciousness. When former Senator Jim Webb (D-VA) introduced legislation to create the National Criminal Justice Commission in 2009, a number of very diverse organizations, from the Major Cities Chiefs Association, the Fraternal Order of Police, the National Sheriffs Association, and the National District Attorneys Association to Human Rights Watch, the American Civil Liberties Union, and the National Association for the Advancement of Colored People all supported it. This legislation would have authorized a national criminal justice commission to conduct a comprehensive review of the criminal justice system by a bipartisan panel of stakeholders, policymakers, and experts that would make thoughtful, evidence-based recommendations for reform. The bill received strong bipartisan support and passed the House but never received a final vote.

More recently, a number of witnesses raised the idea of a national commission at the task force's listening sessions—notably Richard Beary, president of the International Association of Chiefs of Police (IACP), who said,

> For over 20 years, the IACP has called for the creation of a National Commission on Criminal Justice to develop across-the-board improvements to the criminal justice system in order to address current challenges and to increase the efficiency and effectiveness of the entire criminal justice community. A deep dive into community-police relations is only one part of this puzzle. We must explore other aspects of the criminal justice system that need to be revamped and further contribute to today's challenges.[4]

And Jeremy Travis, president of John Jay College of Criminal Justice, added, in the final listening session,

> You said it is time to look at the criminal justice system, and actually I would broaden the scope. We have this question of how to reintegrate into our society those who have caused harms . . . . It is not just the system but these big, democratic, societal questions that go to government functions and how we deal with conflict as well.[5]

---

[3] The President's Commission on Law Enforcement and Administration of Justice, *The Challenge of Crime in a Free Society* (Washington, DC: U.S. Government Printing Office, 1967), 15, https://www.ncjrs.gov/pdffiles1/nij/42.pdf.

[4] Listening Session on Building Trust and Legitimacy (oral testimony of Richard Beary, president, IACP, for the President's Task Force on 21st Century Policing, Washington, DC, January 13–14, 2015).

[5] Listening Session on the Future of Community Policing (oral testimony of Jeremy Travis, president, John Jay College of Criminal Justice, for the President's Task Force on 21st Century Policing, Washington, DC, January 24, 2015).

0.2 OVERARCHING RECOMMENDATION: The President should promote programs that take a comprehensive and inclusive look at community based initiatives that address the core issues of poverty, education, health, and safety.

As is evident from many of the recommendations in this report, the justice system alone cannot solve many of the underlying conditions that give rise to crime. It will be through partnerships across sectors and at every level of government that we will find the effective and legitimate long-term solutions to ensuring public safety.

Pillar One: Building Trust & Legitimacy

Building trust and nurturing legitimacy on both sides of the police/citizen divide is not only the first pillar of this task force's report but also the foundational principle underlying this inquiry into the nature of relations between law enforcement and the communities they serve. For the last two decades, policing has become more effective, better equipped, and better organized to tackle crime. Despite this, Gallup polls show the public's confidence in police work has remained flat, and among some populations of color, confidence has declined.[6] This decline is in addition to the fact that nonwhites have always had less confidence in law enforcement than whites, likely because "the poor and people of color have felt the greatest impact of mass incarceration," such that for "too many poor citizens and people of color, arrest and imprisonment have become an inevitable and seemingly unavoidable part of the American experience."[7] Decades of research and practice support the premise that people are more likely to obey the law when they believe that those who are enforcing it have the legitimate authority to tell them what to do. But the public confers legitimacy only on those whom they believe are acting in procedurally just ways.

Procedurally just behavior is based on four central principles:

1. Treating people with dignity and respect
2. Giving individuals 'voice' during encounters
3. Being neutral and transparent in decision making
4. Conveying trustworthy motives[8]

Research demonstrates that these principles lead to relationships in which the community trusts that officers are honest, unbiased, benevolent, and lawful. The community therefore feels obligated to follow the law and the dictates of legal authorities and is more willing to cooperate with and engage those authorities because it believes that it shares a common set of interests and values with the police.[9]

---

[6] Justin McCarthy, "Nonwhites Less Likely to Feel Police Protect and Serve Them," *Gallup: Politics*, November 17, 2014, http://www.gallup.com/poll/179468/nonwhites-less-likely-feel-police-protect-serve.aspx.

[7] Bryan Stevenson, "Confronting Mass Imprisonment and Restoring Fairness to Collateral Review of Criminal Cases," *Harvard Civil Rights-Civil Liberties Law Review* 41 (Summer 2006): 339–367.

[8] Lorraine Mazerolle, Sarah Bennett, Jacqueline Davis, Elise Sargeant, and Matthew Manning, "Legitimacy in Policing: A Systematic Review," *The Campbell Collection Library of Systematic Reviews* 9 (Oslo, Norway: The Campbell Collaboration, 2013).

[9] Tom Tyler, Jonathon Jackson, and Ben Bradford, "Procedural Justice and Cooperation," in *Encyclopedia of Criminology and Criminal Justice*, eds. Gerben Bruinsma and David Weisburd (New York: Springer, 2014), 4011–4024.

There are both internal and external aspects to procedural justice in policing agencies. Internal procedural justice refers to practices within an agency and the relationships officers have with their colleagues and leaders. Research on internal procedural justice tells us that officers who feel respected by their supervisors and peers are more likely to accept departmental policies, understand decisions, and comply with them voluntarily.[10] It follows that officers who feel respected by their organizations are more likely to bring this respect into their interactions with the people they serve.

External procedural justice focuses on the ways officers and other legal authorities interact with the public and how the characteristics of those interactions shape the public's trust of the police. It is important to understand that a key component of external procedural justice—the practice of fair and impartial policing—is built on understanding and acknowledging human biases,[11] both explicit and implicit.

All human beings have biases or prejudices as a result of their experiences, and these biases influence how they might react when dealing with unfamiliar people or situations. An explicit bias is a conscious bias about certain populations based upon race, gender, socioeconomic status, sexual orientation, or other attributes.[12] Common sense shows that explicit bias is incredibly damaging to police-community relations, and there is a growing body of research evidence that shows that implicit bias—the biases people are not even aware they have—is harmful as well.

Witness Jennifer Eberhardt said,

> Bias is not limited to so-called "bad people." And it certainly is not limited to police officers. The problem is a widespread one that arises from history, from culture, and from racial inequalities that still pervade our society and are especially salient in the context of criminal justice.[13]

To achieve legitimacy, mitigating implicit bias should be a part of training at all levels of a law enforcement organization to increase awareness and ensure respectful encounters both inside the organization and with communities.

---

[10] Nicole Haas et al., "Explaining Officer Compliance: The Importance of Procedural Justice and Trust inside a Police Organization," *Criminology and Criminal Justice* (January 2015), doi: 10.1177/1748895814566288; COPS Office, "Comprehensive Law Enforcement Review: Procedural Justice and Legitimacy," accessed February 28, 2015, http://www.cops.usdoj.gov/pdf/taskforce/Procedural-Justice-and-Legitimacy-LE-Review-Summary.pdf.

[11] Lorie Fridell, "This is Not Your Grandparents' Prejudice: The Implications of the Modern Science of Bias for Police Training," *Translational Criminology* (Fall 2013):10–11.

[12] Susan Fiske, "Are We Born Racist?" *Greater Good* (Summer 2008):14–17.

[13] Listening Session on Building Trust and Legitimacy (oral testimony of Jennifer Eberhardt for the President's Task Force on 21st Century Policing, Washington, DC, January 13, 2015).

The first witnesses at the task force sessions on Pillar One also directly addressed the need for a change in the culture in which police do their work: the use of disrespectful language and the implicit biases that lead officers to rely upon race in the context of stop and frisk. They addressed the need for police officers to find how much they have in common with the people they serve—not the lines of authority they may perceive to separate them—and to continue with enduring programs proven successful over many years.

Several speakers stressed the continuing need for civilian oversight and urged more research into proving ways it can be most effective. And many spoke to the complicated issue of diversity in recruiting, especially Sherrilyn Ifill, who said of youth in poor communities,

> By the time you are 17, you have been stopped and frisked a dozen times. That does not make that 17-year-old want to become a police officer . . . . The challenge is to transform the idea of policing in communities among young people into something they see as honorable. They have to see people at local events, as the person who lives across the street, not someone who comes in and knows nothing about my community.[14]

The task force's specific recommendations that follow offer practical ways agencies can act to promote legitimacy.

1.1 RECOMMENDATION: Law enforcement culture should embrace a guardian mindset to build public trust and legitimacy. Toward that end, police and sheriffs' departments should adopt procedural justice as the guiding principle for internal and external policies and practices to guide their interactions with the citizens they serve.

How officers define their role will set the tone for the community. As Plato wrote, "In a republic that honors the core of democracy—the greatest amount of power is given to those called Guardians. Only those with the most impeccable character are chosen to bear the responsibility of protecting the democracy."

Law enforcement cannot build community trust if it is seen as an occupying force coming in from outside to rule and control the community.

---

[14] Listening Session on Building Trust and Legitimacy (oral testimony of Sherrilyn Ifill, president and director-counsel, NAACP Legal Defense and Educational Fund, Inc., for the President's Task Force on 21st Century Policing, Washington, DC, January 13, 2015); "Statement by the NAACP Legal Defense and Educational Fund, Inc." (written testimony submitted for listening session at Washington, DC, January 13, 2015).

As task force member Susan Rahr wrote

> In 2012, we began asking the question, "Why are we training police officers like soldiers?" Although police officers wear uniforms and carry weapons, the similarity ends there. The missions and rules of engagement are completely different. The soldier's mission is that of a warrior: to conquer. The rules of engagement are decided before the battle. The police officer's mission is that of a guardian: to protect. The rules of engagement evolve as the incident unfolds. Soldiers must follow orders. Police officers must make independent decisions. Soldiers come into communities as an outside, occupying force. Guardians are members of the community, protecting from within.[15]

There's an old saying, "Organizational culture eats policy for lunch." Any law enforcement organization can make great rules and policies that emphasize the guardian role, but if policies conflict with the existing culture, they will not be institutionalized and behavior will not change. In police work, the vast majority of an officer's work is done independently, outside the immediate oversight of a supervisor. But consistent enforcement of rules that conflict with a military-style culture, where obedience to the chain of command is the norm, is nearly impossible. Behavior is more likely to conform to culture than rules.

The culture of policing is also important to the proper exercise of officer discretion and use of authority, as task force member Tracey Meares has written.[16] The values and ethics of the agency will guide officers in their decision-making process; they cannot just rely on rules and policy to act in encounters with the public. Good policing is more than just complying with the law. Sometimes actions are perfectly permitted by policy, but that does not always mean an officer should take those actions. Adopting procedural justice as the guiding principle for internal and external policies and practices can be the underpinning of a change in culture and should contribute to building trust and confidence in the community.

1.2 RECOMMENDATION: Law enforcement agencies should acknowledge the role of policing in past and present injustice and discrimination and how it is a hurdle to the promotion of community trust.

At one listening session, a panel of police chiefs described what they had been doing in recent years to recognize and own the history and to change the culture within both the police forces and the communities.

---

[15] Sue Rahr, "Transforming the Culture of Policing from Warriors to Guardians in Washington State," *International Association of Directors of Law Enforcement Standards and Training Newsletter* 25, no. 4 (2014): 3–4.

[16] Tracey L. Meares, "Rightful Policing," *New Perspectives in Policing Bulletin* (Washington, DC: National Institute of Justice, 2015), NCJ 248411.

Baltimore Police Commissioner Anthony Batts described the process in his city:

> The process started with the commissioning of a study to evaluate the police
> department and the community's views of the agency . . . . The review uncovered
> broken policies, outdated procedures, outmoded technology, and operating norms
> that put officers at odds with the community they are meant to serve. It was clear that
> dramatic and dynamic change was needed.[17]

Ultimately, the Baltimore police created the Professional Standards and Accountability Bureau, tasked with rooting out corruption, holding officers accountable, and implementing national best practices for polices and training. New department heads were appointed and a use of force review structure based on the Las Vegas model was implemented. "These were critical infrastructure changes centered on the need to improve the internal systems that would build accountability and transparency, inside and outside the organization," noted Commissioner Batts.[18]

1.2.1 ACTION ITEM: The U.S. Department of Justice should develop and disseminate case studies that provide examples where past injustices were publically acknowledged by law enforcement agencies in a manner to help build community trust.

1.3 RECOMMENDATION: Law enforcement agencies should establish a culture of transparency and accountability in order to build public trust and legitimacy. This will help ensure decision making is understood and in accord with stated policy.

1.3.1 ACTION ITEM: To embrace a culture of transparency, law enforcement agencies should make all department policies available for public review and regularly post on the department's website information about stops, summonses, arrests, reported crime, and other law enforcement data aggregated by demographics.

1.3.2 ACTION ITEM: When serious incidents occur, including those involving alleged police misconduct, agencies should communicate with citizens and the media swiftly, openly, and neutrally, respecting areas where the law requires confidentiality.

One way to promote neutrality is to ensure that agencies and their members do not release background information on involved parties. While a great deal of information is often publicly available, this information should not be proactively distributed by law enforcement.

---

[17] Listening Session on Community Policing and Crime Reduction: Building Community Policing Organizations (oral testimony of Anthony Batts, commissioner, Baltimore Police Department, for the President's Task Force on 21st Century Policing, Phoenix, AZ, February 13, 2015).

[18] Ibid.

Figure 1. Community members' confidence in their police officers

Photo Removed Due to Copyright Restrictions

Note: Survey conducted August 20–24, 2014. Voluntary responses of "None" and "Don't know/Refused" not shown. Blacks and Whites include only non-Hispanics. Hispanics are of any race.

Source: Jens Manuel Krogstad, "Latino Confidence in Local Police Lower than among Whites," Pew Research Center, August 28, 2014, http://www.pewresearch.org/fact-tank/2014/08/28/latino-confidence-in-local-police-lower-than-among-whites/.

1.4 RECOMMENDATION: Law enforcement agencies should promote legitimacy internally within the organization by applying the principles of procedural justice.

Organizational culture created through employee interaction with management can be linked to officers' interaction with citizens. When an agency creates an environment that promotes internal procedural justice, it encourages its officers to demonstrate external procedural justice. And just as employees are more likely to take direction from management when they believe management's authority is legitimate, citizens are more likely to cooperate with the police when they believe the officers' authority is legitimate.

Internal procedural justice begins with the clear articulation of organizational core values and the transparent creation and fair application of an organization's policies, protocols, and decision-making processes. If the workforce is *actively* involved in policy development, they are more likely to use these same principles of external procedural justice in their interactions with the community. Even though the approach to implementing procedural justice is "top down," the method should include all employees to best reach a shared vision and mission. Research shows that agencies should also use tools that encourage employee and supervisor collaboration and foster strong relationships between supervisors and employees. A more effective agency will result from a real partnership between the chief and the staff and a shared approach to public safety.[19]

1.4.1 ACTION ITEM: In order to achieve internal legitimacy, law enforcement agencies should involve employees in the process of developing policies and procedures.

For example, internal department surveys should ask officers what they think of policing strategies in terms of enhancing or hurting their ability to connect with the public. Sometimes the leadership is out of step with their rank and file, and a survey like this can be a diagnostic tool, a benchmark against which leadership can measure its effectiveness and ability to create a work environment where officers feel safe to discuss their feelings about certain aspects of the job.

1.4.2 ACTION ITEM: Law enforcement agency leadership should examine opportunities to incorporate procedural justice into the internal discipline process, placing additional importance on values adherence rather than adherence to rules. Union leadership should be partners in this process.

1.5 RECOMMENDATION: Law enforcement agencies should proactively promote public trust by initiating positive nonenforcement activities to engage communities that typically have high rates of investigative and enforcement involvement with government agencies.

In communities that have high numbers of interactions with authorities for a variety of reasons, police should actively create opportunities for interactions that are positive and not related to investigation

---

[19] Tim Richardson (senior legislative liaison, Fraternal Order of Police), in discussion with Ajima Olaghere (research assistant, COPS Office, Washington, DC), October 2014.

or enforcement action. Witness Laura Murphy, for example, pointed out how when law enforcement targets people of color for the isolated actions of a few, it tags an entire community as lawless when in actuality 95 percent are law-abiding.[20] This becomes a self-reinforcing concept. Another witness, Carmen Perez, provided an example of police engaging with citizens in another way:

> In the community [where] I grew up in southern California, Oxnard, we had the Police Athletic League. A lot of officers in our communities would volunteer and coach at the police activities league. That became our alternative from violence, from gangs and things like that. That allows for police officers to really build and provide a space to build trusting relationships. No longer was that such and such over there but it was Coach Flores or Coach Brown.[21]

In recent years, agencies across the county have begun to institutionalize community trust building endeavors. They have done this through programs such as Coffee with a Cop (and Sweet Tea with the Chief), Cops and Clergy, Citizens on Patrol Mobile, Students Talking It Over with Police, and The West Side Story Project. Joint community and law dialogues and truth telling, as well as community and law enforcement training in procedural justice and bias, are also occurring nationally. Some agencies are even using training, dialogues, and workshops to take steps towards racial reconciliation.

Agencies engaging in these efforts to build relationships often experience beneficial results. Communities are often more willing to assist law enforcement when agencies need help during investigations. And when critical incidents occur, those agencies already have key allies who can help with information messaging and mitigating challenges.

1.5.1 ACTION ITEM: In order to achieve external legitimacy, law enforcement agencies should involve the community in the process of developing and evaluating policies and procedures.

1.5.2 ACTION ITEM: Law enforcement agencies should institute residency incentive programs such as Resident Officer Programs.

Resident Officer Programs are arrangements where law enforcement officers are provided housing in public housing neighborhoods as long as they fulfill public safety duties within the neighborhood that have been agreed to between the housing authority and the law enforcement agency.

1.5.3 ACTION ITEM: Law enforcement agencies should create opportunities in schools and communities for positive, nonenforcement interactions with police. Agencies should also publicize the beneficial outcomes and images of positive, trust-building partnerships and initiatives.

---

[20] Listening Session on Building Trust and Legitimacy (oral testimony of Laura Murphy to the President's Task Force on 21st Century Policing, Washington, DC, January 13, 2015).

[21] Listening Session on Building Trust and Legitimacy—Community Representatives: Building Community Policing Organizations (oral testimony of Carmen Perez, executive director, The Gathering for Justice, for the President's Task Force on 21st Century Policing, Washington, DC, January 13, 2015).

For example, Michael Reynolds, a member of the Youth and Law Enforcement panel at the Listening Session on Community Policing and Crime Reduction, told the moving story of a police officer who saw him shivering on the street when he was six years old, took him to a store, and bought him a coat. Despite many negative encounters with police since then, the decency and kindness of that officer continue to favorably impact Mr. Reynolds' feelings towards the police.[22]

1.5.4 ACTION ITEM: Use of physical control equipment and techniques against vulnerable populations—including children, elderly persons, pregnant women, people with physical and mental disabilities, limited English proficiency, and others—can undermine public trust and should be used as a last resort. Law enforcement agencies should carefully consider and review their policies towards these populations and adopt policies if none are in place.

1.6 RECOMMENDATION: Law enforcement agencies should consider the potential damage to public trust when implementing crime fighting strategies.

Crime reduction is not self-justifying. Overly aggressive law enforcement strategies can potentially harm communities and do lasting damage to public trust, as numerous witnesses over multiple listening sessions observed.

1.6.1 ACTION ITEM: Research conducted to evaluate the effectiveness of crime fighting strategies should specifically look at the potential for collateral damage of any given strategy on community trust and legitimacy.

1.7 RECOMMENDATION: Law enforcement agencies should track the level of trust in police by their communities just as they measure changes in crime. Annual community surveys, ideally standardized across jurisdictions and with accepted sampling protocols, can measure how policing in that community affects public trust.

Trust in institutions can only be achieved if the public can verify what they are being told about a product or service, who is responsible for the quality of the product or service, and what will be done to correct any problems. To operate effectively, law enforcement agencies must maintain public trust by having a transparent, credible system of accountability.

Agencies should partner with local universities to conduct surveys by ZIP code, for example, to measure the effectiveness of specific policing strategies, assess any negative impact they have on a community's view of police, and gain the community's input.

---

[22] Listening Session on Community Policing and Crime Reduction: Youth and Law Enforcement (oral testimony of Michael Reynolds, co-president, Youth Power Movement, for the President's Task Force on 21st Century Policing, Phoenix, AZ, February 13, 2015).

1.7.1 ACTION ITEM: The Federal Government should develop survey tools and instructions for use of such a model to prevent local departments from incurring the expense and to allow for consistency across jurisdictions.

A model such as the National Institute of Justice-funded National Police Research Platform could be developed and deployed to conduct such surveys. This platform seeks to advance the science and practice of policing in the United States by introducing a new system of measurement and feedback that captures organizational excellence both inside and outside the walls of the agency. The platform is managed by a team of leading police scholars from seven universities supported by the operational expertise of a respected national advisory board.

1.8 RECOMMENDATION: Law enforcement agencies should strive to create a workforce that contains a broad range of diversity including race, gender, language, life experience, and cultural background to improve understanding and effectiveness in dealing with all communities.

Many agencies have long appreciated the critical importance of hiring officers who reflect the communities they serve and also have a high level of procedural justice competency. Achieving diversity in entry level recruiting is important, but achieving systematic and comprehensive diversification throughout each segment of the department is the ultimate goal. It is also important to recognize that diversity means not only race and gender but also the genuine diversity of identity, experience, and background that has been found to help improve the culture of police departments build greater trust and legitimacy with all segments of the population.

A critical factor in managing bias is seeking candidates who are likely to police in an unbiased manner.[23] Since people are less likely to have biases against groups with which they have had positive experiences, police departments should seek candidates who have had positive interactions with people of various cultures and backgrounds.[24]

1.8.1 ACTION ITEM: The Federal Government should create a Law Enforcement Diversity Initiative designed to help communities diversify law enforcement departments to reflect the demographics of the community.

1.8.2 ACTION ITEM: The department overseeing this initiative should help localities learn best practices for recruitment, training, and outreach to improve the diversity as well as the cultural and linguistic responsiveness of law enforcement agencies.

National and local affinity police organizations could be formally included in this effort. This program should also evaluate and assess diversity among law enforcement agencies around the country and issue public reports on national trends.

---

[23] Lorie Fridell, "Racially Biased Policing: The Law Enforcement Response to the Implicit Black-Crime Association," in *Racial Divide: Racial and Ethnic Bias in the Criminal Justice System,* eds. Michael J. Lynch, E. Britt Patterson, and Kristina K. Childs (Monsey, NY: Criminal Justice Press, 2008), 51.

[24] Ibid., 51–52.

1.8.3 ACTION ITEM: Successful law enforcement agencies should be highlighted and celebrated and those with less diversity should be offered technical assistance to facilitate change.

Law enforcement agencies must be continuously creative with recruitment efforts and employ the public, business, and civic communities to help.

1.8.4 ACTION ITEM: Discretionary federal funding for law enforcement programs could be influenced by that department's efforts to improve their diversity and cultural and linguistic responsiveness.

1.8.5 ACTION ITEM: Law enforcement agencies should be encouraged to explore more flexible staffing models.

As is common in the nursing profession, offering flexible schedules can help officers achieve better work-life balance that attracts and encourages retention, particularly for officers with sole responsibility for the care of family members.

1.9 RECOMMENDATION: Law enforcement agencies should build relationships based on trust with immigrant communities. This is central to overall public safety.

Immigrants often fear approaching police officers when they are victims of and witnesses to crimes and when local police are entangled with federal immigration enforcement. At all levels of government, it is important that laws, policies, and practices do not hinder the ability of local law enforcement to build the strong relationships necessary to public safety and community well-being. It is the view of this task force that whenever possible, state and local law enforcement should not be involved in immigration enforcement.

1.9.1 ACTION ITEM: Decouple federal immigration enforcement from routine local policing for civil enforcement and nonserious crime.

The U.S. Department of Homeland Security should terminate the use of the state and local criminal justice system, including through detention, notification and transfer requests, to enforce civil immigration laws against civil and nonserious criminal offenders.[25]

In 2011, the Major Cities Chiefs Association recommended nine points to Congress and the President on this issue, noting that "immigration is a federal policy issue between the United States government and other countries, not local or state entities and other countries. Any immigration enforcement laws or practices should be nationally based, consistent, and federally funded."[26]

---

[25] Listening Session on Building Trust and Legitimacy: Civil Rights/Civil Liberties (oral testimony of Maria Teresa Kumar, president and CEO, Voto Latino, for the President's Task Force on 21st Century Policing, Washington, DC, January 13, 2015).

[26] "Major Cities Chiefs Association Immigration Position October 2011," accessed February 26, 2015, http://majorcitieschiefs.com/pdf/news/immigration_position112811.pdf.

1.9.2 ACTION ITEM: Law enforcement agencies should ensure reasonable and equitable language access for all persons who have encounters with police or who enter the criminal justice system.[27]

1.9.3 ACTION ITEM: The U.S. Department of Justice should remove civil immigration information from the FBI's National Crime Information Center database.[28]

---

[27] Listening Session on Building Trust and Legitimacy (written testimony of Nicholas Turner, president and director, Vera Institute of Justice, for the President's Task Force on 21st Century Policing, Washington, DC, January 13, 2015).

[28] Listening Session on Community Policing and Crime Reduction (written testimony of Javier Valdes, executive director, Make the Road New York, for the President's Task Force on 21st Century Policing, Phoenix, AZ, February 13–14, 2015).

Pillar Two: Policy & Oversight

The issues addressed in Pillar One of this report, building trust and legitimacy between law enforcement agencies and the communities they serve, underlie all questions of law enforcement policy and community oversight. If police are to carry out their responsibilities according to established policies, these policies must be reflective of community values and not lead to practices that result in disparate impacts on various segments of the community. They also need to be clearly articulated to the community and implemented transparently so police will have credibility with residents and the people can have faith that their guardians are always acting in their best interests.

Paramount among the policies of law enforcement organizations are those controlling use of force. Not only should there be policies for deadly and nondeadly uses of force but a clearly stated "sanctity of life" philosophy must also be in the forefront of every officer's mind. This way of thinking should be accompanied by rigorous practical ongoing training in an atmosphere of nonjudgmental and safe sharing of views with fellow officers about how they behaved in use of force situations. At one listening session, Geoffrey Alpert described Officer-Created Jeopardy Training, in which officers who had been in situations where mistakes were made or force was used came to explain their decision making to other officers. Some explained what they did right and how potentially violent situations were resolved without violence. Other officers told what they did wrong, why they made mistakes, what information was missing or misinterpreted, and how they could have improved their behavior and response to suspects.[29]

Data collection, supervision, and accountability are also part of a comprehensive systemic approach to keeping everyone safe and protecting the rights of all involved during police encounters. Members of the Division of Policing of the American Society of Criminology recently wrote, "While the United States presently employs a broad array of social and economic indicators in order to gauge the overall 'health' of the nation, it has a much more limited set of indicators concerning the behavior of the police and the quality of law enforcement."[30]

That body noted that Section 210402 of the Violent Crime Control and Law Enforcement Act of 1994 requires the U.S. Attorney General to "acquire data about the use of excessive force by law enforcement officers" and to "publish an annual summary of the data acquired under this section."[31] But the U.S. Department of Justice (DOJ) has never been allocated the funds necessary to undertake the serious and sustained program of research and development to fulfill this mandate. Expanded

---

[29] Listening Session on Policy and Oversight: Use of Force Research and Policies (oral testimony of Geoffrey Alpert, professor, University of South Carolina, for the President's Task Force on 21st Century Policing, Cincinnati, OH, January 30, 2015).

[30] "Recommendations to the President's Task Force on 21st Century Policing," Listening Session on Training and Education (written testimony of Anthony Braga et al., Ad Hoc Committee to the President's Task Force on 21st Century Policing, Division of Policing, American Society of Criminology, February 13–14, 2015).

[31] Ibid.

research and data collection are also necessary to knowing what works and what does not work, which policing practices are effective and which ones have unintended consequences. Greater acceptance of the Federal Bureau of Investigation's (FBI) National Incident-Based Reporting System could also benefit policing practice and research endeavors.

Mass demonstrations, for example, are occasions where evidence-based practices successfully applied can make the difference between a peaceful demonstration and a riot. Citizens have a Constitutional right to freedom of expression, including the right to peacefully demonstrate. There are strong examples of proactive and positive communication and engagement strategies that can protect constitutional rights of demonstrators and the safety of citizens and the police.[32]

2.1 RECOMMENDATION: Law enforcement agencies should collaborate with community members to develop policies and strategies in communities and neighborhoods disproportionately affected by crime for deploying resources that aim to reduce crime by improving relationships, greater community engagement, and cooperation.

The development of a service model process that focuses on the root causes of crime should include the community members themselves because what works in one neighborhood might not be equally successful in every other one. Larger departments could commit resources and personnel to areas of high poverty, limited services, and at-risk or vulnerable populations through creating priority units with specialized training and added status and pay. Chief Charlie Beck of the Los Angeles Police Department (LAPD) described the LAPD's Community Safety Partnership, in which officers engage the community and build trust where it is needed most, in the public housing projects in Watts. The department has assigned 45 officers to serve for five years at three housing projects in Watts and at an additional housing project in East Los Angeles. Through a partnership with the Advancement Project and the Housing Authority of the City of Los Angeles, the program involves officers going into the housing developments with the intent *not* to make arrests but to create partnerships, create relationships, hear the community, and see what they need—and then work together to make those things happen.[33]

2.1.1 ACTION ITEM: The Federal Government should incentivize this collaboration through a variety of programs that focus on public health, education, mental health, and other programs not traditionally part of the criminal justice system.

---

[32] Listening Session on Policy and Oversight: Mass Demonstrations (oral testimony of Garry McCarthy, chief of police, Chicago Police Department, for the President's Task Force on 21st Century Policing, Cincinnati, OH, January 31, 2015); Listening Session on Policy and Oversight: Mass Demonstrations (oral testimony of Rodney Monroe, chief of police, Charlotte-Mecklenberg [NC] Police Department, for the President's Task Force on 21st Century Policing, Cincinnati, OH, January 30, 2015).

[33] Listening Session on Policy and Oversight: Civilian Oversight (oral testimony of Charlie Beck, chief, Los Angeles Police Department, for the President's Task Force on 21st Century Policing, Cincinnati, OH, January 30, 2015).

2.2 RECOMMENDATION: Law enforcement agencies should have comprehensive policies on the use of force that include training, investigations, prosecutions, data collection, and information sharing. These policies must be clear, concise, and openly available for public inspection.

2.2.1 ACTION ITEM: Law enforcement agency policies for training on use of force should emphasize de-escalation and alternatives to arrest or summons in situations where appropriate.

As Chuck Wexler noted in his testimony,

> In traditional police culture, officers are taught never to back down from a confrontation, but instead to run *toward* the dangerous situation that everyone else is running away from. However, sometimes the best tactic for dealing with a minor confrontation is to step back, call for assistance, de-escalate, and perhaps plan a different enforcement action that can be taken more safely later.[34]

Policies should also include, at a minimum, annual training that includes shoot/don't shoot scenarios and the use of less than lethal technologies.

2.2.2 ACTION ITEM: These policies should also mandate external and independent criminal investigations in cases of police use of force resulting in death, officer-involved shootings resulting in injury or death, or in-custody deaths.

One way this can be accomplished is by the creation of multi-agency force investigation task forces comprising state and local investigators. Other ways to structure this investigative process include referring to neighboring jurisdictions or to the next higher levels of government (many smaller departments may already have state agencies handle investigations), but in order to restore and maintain trust, this independence is crucial.

In written testimony to the task force, James Palmer of the Wisconsin Professional Police Association offered an example in that state's statutes requiring that agency written policies "require an investigation that is conducted by at least two investigators . . . neither of whom is employed by a law enforcement agency that employs a law enforcement officer involved in the officer-involved death."[35] Furthermore, in order to establish and maintain internal legitimacy and procedural justice, these investigations should be performed by law enforcement agencies with adequate training, knowledge, and experience investigating police use of force.

---

[34] Listening Session on Policy and Oversight: Use of Force Investigations and Oversight (oral testimony of Chuck Wexler, executive director, Police Executive Research Forum, for the President's Task Force on 21st Century Policing, Cincinnati, OH, January 30, 2015).

[35] Listening Session on Policy and Oversight (written testimony of James Palmer, executive director, Wisconsin Professional Police Association, for the President's Task Force on 21st Century Policing, Cincinnati, OH, January 30–31, 2015).

2.2.3 ACTION ITEM: The task force encourages policies that mandate the use of external and independent prosecutors in cases of police use of force resulting in death, officer-involved shootings resulting in injury or death, or in-custody deaths.

Strong systems and policies that encourage use of an independent prosecutor for reviewing police uses of force and for prosecution in cases of inappropriate deadly force and in-custody death will demonstrate the transparency to the public that can lead to mutual trust between community and law enforcement.

2.2.4 ACTION ITEM: Policies on use of force should also require agencies to collect, maintain, and report data to the Federal Government on all officer-involved shootings, whether fatal or nonfatal, as well as any in-custody death.

In-custody deaths are not only deaths in a prison or jail but also deaths that occur in the process of an arrest. The Bureau of Justice Statistics (BJS) implemented the Arrest Related Deaths data collection in 2003 as part of requirements set forth in the Deaths in Custody Reporting Act of 2000 and reenacted in 2014, but this is a voluntary reporting program. Access to this data is important to gain a national picture of police use of force as well as to incentivize the systematic and transparent collection and analysis of use of force incident data at the local level. The reported data should include information on the circumstances of the use of force, as well as the race, gender, and age of the decedents. Data should be reported to the U.S. Department of Justice through the FBI's Uniform Crime Reporting System or an expansion of collections managed by the BJS.

2.2.5 ACTION ITEM: Policies on use of force should clearly state what types of information will be released, when, and in what situation, to maintain transparency.

This should also include procedures on the release of a summary statement regarding the circumstances of the incident by the department as soon as possible and within 24 hours. The intent of this directive should be to share as much information as possible without compromising the integrity of the investigation or anyone's rights.

2.2.6 ACTION ITEM: Law enforcement agencies should establish a Serious Incident Review Board comprising sworn staff and community members to review cases involving officer involved shootings and other serious incidents that have the potential to damage community trust or confidence in the agency. The purpose of this board should be to identify any administrative, supervisory, training, tactical, or policy issues that need to be addressed.

2.3 RECOMMENDATION: Law enforcement agencies are encouraged to implement nonpunitive peer review of critical incidents separate from criminal and administrative investigations.

These reviews, sometimes known as "near miss" or "sentinel event" reviews, focus on the improvement of practices and policy. Such reviews already exist in medicine, aviation, and other industries. According to the National Institute of Justice (NIJ), a sentinel event in criminal justice would include wrongful convictions but also "near miss" acquittals and dismissals of cases that at earlier points seemed solid; cold cases that stayed cold too long; wrongful releases of dangerous or factually guilty criminals or of vulnerable arrestees with mental disabilities; and failures to prevent domestic violence within at-risk families.

Sentinel events can include episodes that are within policy but disastrous in terms of community relations, whether or not everyone agrees that the event should be classified as an error. In fact, anything that stakeholders agree can cause widespread or viral attention could be considered a sentinel event.[36]

What distinguishes sentinel event reviews from other kinds of internal investigations of apparent errors is that they are nonadversarial. As task force member Sean Smoot has written,

> For sentinel event reviews to be effective and practical, they must be cooperative efforts that afford the types of protections provided in the medical context, where state and federal laws protect the privacy of participants and prevent the disclosure of information to anyone outside of the sentinel event review . . . . Unless the sentinel event process is honest and trustworthy, with adequate legal protections—including use immunity, privacy, confidentiality, and nondisclosure, for example—police officers, who have the very best information about how things really work and what really happened, will not be motivated to fully participate. The sentinel event review approach will have a better chance of success if departments can abandon the process of adversarial/punitive-based discipline, adopting instead "education-based" disciplinary procedures and policies.[37]

2.4 RECOMMENDATION: Law enforcement agencies are encouraged to adopt identification procedures that implement scientifically supported practices that eliminate or minimize presenter bias or influence.

A recent study by the National Academy of Sciences, *Identifying the Culprit: Assessing Eyewitness Identification*, studied the important role played by eyewitnesses in criminal cases, noting that research on factors affecting the accuracy of eyewitness identification procedures has given an increasingly clear picture of how identifications are made and, more important, an improved understanding of the limits on vision and memory that can lead to failure of identification.[38] Many factors, including external conditions and the witness's emotional state and biases, influence what a

---

[36] James M. Doyle, "Learning from Error in the Criminal Justice System: Sentinel Event Reviews," *Mending Justice: Sentinel Event Reviews* (Special Report from the National Institute of Justice, September 2014): 3–20.

[37] Sean Smoot, "Punishment-Based vs. Education-Based Discipline: A Surmountable Challenge?" in *Mending Justice: Sentinel Event Reviews* (Special Report from the National Institute of Justice, September 2014): 48–50.

[38] Samuel R. Gross et al., "Rate of False Conviction of Criminal Defendants who are Sentenced to Death," Proceedings of the National Academy of Sciences of the United States of America 111, no. 20 (2014): 7230–7235. http://www.pnas.org/content/111/20/7230.full.pdf+html.

witness sees or thinks she sees. Memories can be forgotten, reconstructed, updated, and distorted. Meanwhile, policies governing law enforcement procedures for conducting and recording identifications are not standard, and policies and practices to address the issue of misidentification vary widely.

2.5 RECOMMENDATION: All federal, state, local, and tribal law enforcement agencies should report and make available to the public census data regarding the composition of their departments including race, gender, age, and other relevant demographic data.

While the BJS collects information on many aspects of police activities, there is no single data collection instrument that yields the information requested in this recommendation. Demographic data should be collected and made available to the public so communities can assess the diversity of their departments and do so in a national context. This data will also be important to better understand the impact of diversity on the functioning of departments. Malik Aziz, National Chair of the National Black Police Association (NBPA), reminded the task force that the NBPA not only urges all departments to meet the demographics of the community in which they serve by maintaining a plan of action to recruit and retain police officers of color but also has called for the DOJ to collect the annual demographic statistics from the 18,000 police agencies across the nation. "It is not enough to mandate diversity," he stated, "but it becomes necessary to diversify command ranks in departments that have historically failed to develop and/or promote qualified and credentialed officers to executive and command ranks."[39]

2.5.1 ACTION ITEM: The Bureau of Justice Statistics should add additional demographic questions to the Law Enforcement Management and Administrative Statistics (LEMAS) survey in order to meet the intent of this recommendation.

2.6 RECOMMENDATION: Law enforcement agencies should be encouraged to collect, maintain, and analyze demographic data on all detentions (stops, frisks, searches, summons, and arrests). This data should be disaggregated by school and non-school contacts.

The BJS periodically conducts the Police-Public Contact Survey, a supplement to the National Crime Victimization Survey. The most recent survey, released in 2013, asked a nationally representative sample of U.S. residents age 16 or older about experiences with police during the prior 12 months.[40] But these surveys do not reflect what is happening every day at the local level when police interact with members of the communities they serve. More research and tools along the lines of Lorie Fridell's

---

[39] Listening Session on Policy and Oversight: Law Enforcement Culture and Diversity (oral testimony of Malik Aziz, chairman, National Black Police Association, for the President's Task Force on 21st Century Policing, Cincinnati, OH, January 30, 2015).

[40] Lynn Langton and Matthew Durose, *Police Behavior during Traffic and Street Stops, 2011,* Special Report (Washington, DC: Office of Justice Programs Bureau of Justice Statistics, 2013), NCJ 242937; Matthew Durose and Lynn Langton, *Requests for Police Assistance, 2011,* Special Report (Washington, DC: Office of Justice Programs Bureau of Justice Statistics, 2013), NCJ 242938.

2004 publication, *By the Numbers: A Guide for Analyzing Race Data From Vehicle Stops*—to help local agencies collect and analyze their data, understand the importance of context to the analysis and reporting process, and establish benchmarks resulting from their findings—would improve understanding and lead to evidence-based policies.

2.6.1 ACTION ITEM: The Federal Government could further incentivize universities and other organizations to partner with police departments to collect data and develop knowledge about analysis and benchmarks as well as to develop tools and templates that help departments manage data collection and analysis.

2.7 RECOMMENDATION: Law enforcement agencies should create policies and procedures for policing mass demonstrations that employ a continuum of managed tactical resources that are designed to minimize the appearance of a military operation and avoid using provocative tactics and equipment that undermine civilian trust.

Policies should emphasize protection of the First Amendment rights of demonstrators and effective ways of communicating with them. Superintendent Garry McCarthy of the Chicago Police Department detailed his police force training and operations in advance of the 2012 NATO Summit at the height of the "Occupy" movement. The department was determined not to turn what it knew would be a mass demonstration into a riot. Police officers refreshed "perishable" skills, such as engaging in respectful conversations with demonstrators, avoiding confrontation, and using "extraction techniques" not only on the minority of demonstrators who were behaving unlawfully (throwing rocks, etc.) but also on officers who were becoming visibly upset and at risk of losing their composure and professional demeanor.[41]

2.7.1. ACTION ITEM: Law enforcement agency policies should address procedures for implementing a layered response to mass demonstrations that prioritize de-escalation and a guardian mindset.

These policies could include plans to minimize confrontation by using "soft look" uniforms, having officers remove riot gear as soon as practical, and maintaining open postures. "When officers line up in a military formation while wearing full protective gear, their visual appearance may have a dramatic influence on how the crowd perceives them and how the event ends."[42]

2.7.2 ACTION ITEM: The Federal Government should create a mechanism for investigating complaints and issuing sanctions regarding the inappropriate use of equipment and tactics during mass demonstrations.

---

[41] Listening Session on Policy and Oversight (oral testimony of Garry McCarthy, Chicago Police Department, to the President's Task Force on 21st Century Policing, Cincinnati, OH, January 30, 2015).

[42] Listening Session on Policy and Oversight (written testimony of Edward MacGuire, American University, for the President's Task Force on 21st Century Policing, Cincinnati, OH, January 30, 2015).

There has been substantial media attention in recent months surrounding the police use of military equipment at events where members of the public are exercising their First Amendment rights. This has led to the creation of the President's Interagency Law Enforcement Equipment Working Group.

This group has been tasked by the Executive Order of January 16, 2015 with a number of issues, including ensuring that law enforcement agencies adopt organizational and operational practices and standards that prevent the misuse or abuse of controlled equipment and ensuring compliance with civil rights requirements resulting from receipt of federal financial assistance.

2.8 RECOMMENDATION: Some form of civilian oversight of law enforcement is important in order to strengthen trust with the community. Every community should define the appropriate form and structure of civilian oversight to meet the needs of that community.

Many, but not all, state and local agencies operate with the oversight or input of civilian police boards or commissions. Part of the process of assessing the need and desire for new or additional civilian oversight should include input from and collaboration with police employees because the people to be overseen should be part of the process that will oversee them. This guarantees that the principles of internal procedural justice are in place to benefit both the police and the community they serve.

We must examine civilian oversight in the communities where it operates and determine which models are successful in promoting police and community understanding. There are important arguments for having civilian oversight even though we lack strong research evidence that it works. Therefore we urge action on further research, based on the guiding principle of procedural justice, to find evidence-based practices to implement successful civilian oversight mechanisms.

As noted by witness Brian Buchner at the Policy and Oversight Listening Session on January 30,

> Citizen review is not an advocate for the community or for the police. This impartiality allows oversight to bring stakeholders together to work collaboratively and proactively to help make policing more effective and responsive to the community. Civilian oversight alone is not sufficient to gain legitimacy; without it, however, it is difficult, if not impossible, for the police to maintain the public's trust.[43]

2.8.1 ACTION ITEM: The U.S. Department of Justice, through its research arm, the National Institute of Justice (NIJ), should expand its research agenda to include civilian oversight.

NIJ recently announced its research priorities in policing for FY 2015, which include such topics as police use of force, body-worn cameras, and procedural justice. While proposals related to research on police oversight might fit into several of these topical areas, police oversight is not highlighted by NIJ in

---

[43] Listening Session on Policy and Oversight (oral testimony of Brian Buchner, president, National Association for Civilian Oversight of Law Enforcement, for the President's Task Force on 21st Century Policing, Cincinnati, OH, January 30, 2015).

any of them. NIJ should specifically invite research into civilian oversight and its impact on and relationship to policing in one or more of these areas.

2.8.2 ACTION ITEM: The U.S. Department of Justice's Office of Community Oriented Policing Services (COPS Office) should provide technical assistance and collect best practices from existing civilian oversight efforts and be prepared to help cities create this structure, potentially with some matching grants and funding.

2.9 RECOMMENDATION: Law enforcement agencies and municipalities should refrain from practices requiring officers to issue a predetermined number of tickets, citations, arrests, or summonses, or to initiate investigative contacts with citizens for reasons not directly related to improving public safety, such as generating revenue.

Productivity expectations can be effective performance management tools. But testimony from Laura Murphy, Director of the Washington Legislative Office of the American Civil Liberties Union, identifies some of the negative effects of these practices:

> One only needs to paint a quick picture of the state of policing to understand the dire need for reform. First, there are local and federal incentives that instigate arrests. At the local level, cities across the country generate much of their revenue through court fines and fees, with those who can't pay subject to arrest and jail time. These debtors' prisons are found in cities like Ferguson, where the number of arrest warrants in 2013—33,000—exceeded its population of 21,000. Most of the warrants were for driving violations.[44]

2.10 RECOMMENDATION: Law enforcement officers should be required to seek consent before a search and explain that a person has the right to refuse consent when there is no warrant or probable cause. Furthermore, officers should ideally obtain written acknowledgement that they have sought consent to a search in these circumstances.

2.11 RECOMMENDATION: Law enforcement agencies should establish search and seizure procedures related to LGBTQ and transgender populations and adopt as policy the recommendation from the President's HIV/AIDS Task Force to cease using the possession of condoms as the sole evidence of vice.

---

[44] Listening Session on Trust and Legitimacy (oral testimony of Laura Murphy, director of the Washington Legislative Office, American Civil Liberties Union, for the President's Task Force on 21st Century Policing, Washington, DC, January 13, 2015); Joseph Shapiro, "In Ferguson, Court Fines and Fees Fuel Anger," NPR.com, last updated August 25, 2014, http://www.npr.org/2014/08/25/343143937/in-ferguson-court-fines-and-fees-fuel-anger; *In For A Penny: The Rise of America's Debtors' Prisons* (New York: American Civil Liberties Union, 2010), http://www.aclu.org/files/assets/InForAPenny_web.pdf.

2.12 RECOMMENDATION: Law enforcement agencies should adopt and enforce policies prohibiting profiling and discrimination based on race, ethnicity, national origin, age, gender, gender identity/expression, sexual orientation, immigration status, disability, housing status, occupation, and/or language fluency.

The task force heard from a number of witnesses about the importance of protecting the safety and dignity of all people. Andrea Ritchie noted that

> Gender and sexuality-specific forms of racial profiling and discriminatory policing [include] . . . . Failure to respect individuals' gender identity and expression when addressing members of the public and during arrest processing, searches, and placement in police custody.[45]

Invasive searches should never be used for the sole purpose of determining gender identity, and an individual's gender identity should be respected in lock-ups and holding cells to the extent that the facility allows for gender segregation. And witness Linda Sarsour spoke to how

> an issue plaguing and deeply impacting Arab-American and American Muslim communities across the country is racial and religious profiling by local, state, and federal law enforcement. We have learned through investigative reports, Freedom of Information Act (FOIA) requests, and lawsuits that agencies target communities by religion and national origin.[46]

2.12.1 ACTION ITEM: The Bureau of Justice Statistics should add questions concerning sexual harassment of and misconduct toward LGBTQ and gender-nonconforming people by law enforcement officers to the Police Public Contact Survey.

2.12.2 ACTION ITEM: The Centers for Disease Control should add questions concerning sexual harassment of and misconduct toward LGBTQ and gender-nonconforming people by law enforcement officers to the National Intimate Partner and Sexual Violence Survey.

2.12.3 ACTION ITEM: The U.S. Department of Justice should promote and disseminate guidance to federal, state, and local law enforcement agencies on documenting, preventing, and addressing sexual harassment and misconduct by local law enforcement agents, consistent with the recommendations of the International Association of Chiefs of Police.[47]

---

[45] Listening Session on Training and Education (oral testimony of Andrea Ritchie, founder of Streetwise and Safe, for the President's Task Force on 21st Century Policing, Phoenix, AZ, February 14, 2015).

[46] Listening Session on Training and Education (oral testimony of Linda Sarsour, Advocacy And Civic Engagement coordinator for the National Network for Arab American Communities, for the President's Task Force on 21st Century Policing, Phoenix, AZ, February 14, 2015).

[47] IACP, *Addressing Sexual Offenses and Misconduct by Law Enforcement: Executive Guide* (Alexandria, VA: International Association of Chiefs of Police, 2011).

2.13 RECOMMENDATION: The U.S. Department of Justice, through the Office of Community Oriented Policing Services and Office of Justice Programs, should provide technical assistance and incentive funding to jurisdictions with small police agencies that take steps towards shared services, regional training, and consolidation.

Half of all law enforcement agencies in the United States have fewer than ten officers, and nearly three-quarters have fewer than 25 officers.[48] Lawrence Sherman noted in his testimony that "so many problems of organizational quality control are made worse by the tiny size of most local police agencies . . . less than 1 percent of 17,985 U.S. police agencies meet the English minimum of 1,000 employees or more."[49] These small forces often lack the resources for training and equipment accessible to larger departments and often are prevented by municipal boundaries and local custom from combining forces with neighboring agencies. Funding and technical assistance can give smaller agencies the incentive to share policies and practices and give them access to a wider variety of training, equipment, and communications technology than they could acquire on their own.

Table 1. Full-time state and local law enforcement employees, by size of agency, 2008

Size of agency*	Number of agencies	Total number of full-time employees
All agencies	17,985	1,133,915
1,000 or more officers	83	326,197
500–999	89	94,168
250–499	237	133,024
100–249	778	174,505
50–99	1,300	136,390
25–49	2,402	124,492
10–24	4,300	98,563
5–9	3,446	32,493
2–4	3,225	11,498
0–1	2,125	2,585

Source: Brian A. Reaves, "Census of State and Local Law Enforcement Agencies, 2008,"Bulletin (Washington, DC: Bureau of Justice Statistics, July 2011), http://www.bjs.gov/content/pub/pdf/csllea08.pdf.

---

[48] Brian A. Reaves, *Census of State and Local Law Enforcement Agencies, 2008,* Bulletin (Washington, DC: Office of Justice Programs Bureau of Justice Statistics, 2011), NCJ 233982.

[49] Listening Session on the Future of Community Policing (oral testimony of Lawrence Sherman, Cambridge University, for the President's Task Force on 21st Century Policing, Washington, DC, February 24, 2015).

2.14 RECOMMENDATION: The U.S. Department of Justice, through the Office of Community Oriented Policing Services, should partner with the International Association of Directors of Law Enforcement Standards and Training (IADLEST) to expand its National Decertification Index to serve as the National Register of Decertified Officers with the goal of covering all agencies within the United States and its territories.

The National Decertification Index is an aggregation of information that allows hiring agencies to identify officers who have had their license or certification revoked for misconduct. It was designed as an answer to the problem "wherein a police officer is discharged for improper conduct and loses his/her certification in that state . . . [only to relocate] to another state and hire on with another police department."[50] Peace Officer Standards and Training (POST) boards can record administrative actions taken against certified police and correctional officers. Currently the criteria for reporting an action on an officer is determined by each POST independently, as is the granting of read-only access to hiring departments to use as part of their pre-hire screening process. Expanding this system to ensure national and standardized reporting would assist in ensuring that officers who have lost their certification for misconduct are not easily hired in other jurisdictions. A national register would effectively treat "police professionals the way states' licensing laws treat other professionals. If anything, the need for such a system is even more important for law enforcement, as officers have the power to make arrests, perform searches, and use deadly force."[51]

2.15 RECOMMENDATION: Law enforcement agencies should adopt policies requiring officers to provide their names to individuals they have stopped, along with the reason for the stop, the reason for a search if one is conducted, and a card with information on how to reach the civilian complaint review board.

---

[50] "National Decertification Index—FAQs," accessed February 27, 2015, https://www.iadlest.org/Portals/0/Files/NDI/FAQ/ndi_faq.html.

[51] Roger L. Goldman, "Police Officer Decertification: Promoting Police Professionalism through State Licensing and the National Decertification Index," *Police Chief* 81 (November 2014): 40–42, http://www.policechiefmagazine.org/magazine/index.cfm?fuseaction=display_arch&article_id=3538&issue_id=1 12014.

Pillar Three: Technology & Social Media

We live in a time when technology and its many uses are advancing far more quickly than are policies and laws. "Technology" available to law enforcement today includes everything from body-worn cameras (BWC) to unmanned aircraft to social media and a myriad of products in between.

The use of technology can improve policing practices and build community trust and legitimacy, but its implementation must be built on a defined policy framework with its purposes and goals clearly delineated. Implementing new technologies can give police departments an opportunity to fully engage and educate communities in a dialogue about their expectations for transparency, accountability, and privacy. But technology changes quickly in terms of new hardware, software, and other options. Law enforcement agencies and leaders need to be able to identify, assess, and evaluate new technology for adoption and do so in ways that improve their effectiveness, efficiency, and evolution without infringing on individual rights.

Thus, despite (and because of) the centrality of technology in policing, law enforcement agencies face major challenges including determining the effects of implementing various technologies; identifying costs and benefits; examining unintended consequences; and exploring the best practices by which technology can be evaluated, acquired, maintained, and managed. Addressing these technology challenges by using research, accumulated knowledge, and practical experiences can help agencies reach their goals,[52] but law enforcement agencies and personnel also need to recognize that technology is only a tool for doing their jobs: just because you have access to technology does not necessarily mean you should always use it.[53]

BWCs are a case in point. An increasing number of law enforcement agencies are adopting BWC programs as a means to improve evidence collection, to strengthen officer performance and accountability, and to enhance agency transparency. By documenting encounters between police and the public, BWCs can also be used to investigate and resolve complaints about officer-involved incidents.

Jim Bueermann, retired chief of the Redlands (California) Police Department and President of the Police Foundation, told the task force about a seminal piece of research that demonstrated a positive impact of BWCs in policing. The researchers used the gold standard of research models, a randomized

---

[52] Elizabeth Groff and Tom McEwen, *Identifying and Measuring the Effects of Information Technologies on Law Enforcement Agencies: The Making Officer Redeployment Effective Program* (Washington, DC: Office of Community Oriented Policing Services, 2008), http://www.cops.usdoj.gov/Publications/e08084156-IT.pdf; Christopher S. Koper, Cynthia Lum, James J. Willis, Daniel J. Woods, and Julie Hibdon, *Realizing the Potential of Technology in Policing: A Multi-Site Study of the Social, Organizational, and Behavioral Aspects of Implementing Police Technologies* (Washington, DC: National Institute of Justice, 2015), http://cebcp.org/wp-content/evidence-based-policing/ImpactTechnologyFinalReport.

[53] IACP Technology Policy Framework (Alexandria, VA: International Association of Chiefs of Police, 2014), http://www.theiacp.org/Portals/0/documents/pdfs/IACP%20Technology%20Policy%20Framework%20January%202014%20Final.pdf.

control trial, in which the people being studied are randomly assigned either to a control group that does not receive the treatment being studied or to a treatment group that does. The results of this 12-month study are highly suggestive that the use of BWCs by the police can significantly reduce both officer use of force and complaints against officers. They found that the officers wearing the cameras had 87.5 percent fewer incidents of use of force and 59 percent fewer complaints than the officers not wearing the cameras. One of the important findings of the study was the impact BWCs might have on the self-awareness of officers and citizens alike. When police officers are acutely aware that their behavior is being monitored (because they turn on the cameras), and when officers tell citizens that the cameras are recording their behavior, everyone behaves better. The results of this study are highly suggestive that this increase in self-awareness contributes to more positive outcomes in police-citizen interaction.[54]

But other considerations make the issue of BWCs more complex. A 2014 Police Executive Research Forum (PERF) publication, funded by the Office of Community Oriented Policing Services (COPS Office), reporting on extensive research exploring the policy and implementation questions surrounding BWCs noted,

> Although body-worn cameras can offer many benefits, they also raise serious questions about how technology is changing the relationship between police and the community. Body-worn cameras not only create concerns about the public's privacy rights but also can affect how officers relate to people in the community, the community's perception of the police, and expectations about how police agencies should share information with the public.[55]

Now that agencies operate in a world in which anyone with a cell phone camera can record video footage of a police encounter, BWCs help police departments ensure that events are also captured from an officer's perspective.[56] But when the public does not believe its privacy is being protected by law enforcement, a breakdown in community trust can occur. Agencies need to consider ways to involve the public in discussions related to the protection of their privacy and civil liberties prior to implementing new technology, as well work with the public and other partners in the justice system to develop appropriate policies and procedures for use.

Another technology relatively new to law enforcement is social media. Social media is a communication tool the police can use to engage the community on issues of importance to both and

---

[54] Listening Session on Technology and Social Media: Body Cameras-Research and Legal Considerations (oral testimony of Jim Bueermann, president, Police Foundation, for the President's Task Force on 21st Century Policing, Cincinnati, OH, January 31, 2015); Ariel Barak, William A. Farrar, and Alex Sutherland, "The Effect of Police Body-Worn Cameras on Use of Force and Citizens' Complaints Against the Police: A Randomized Controlled Trial," *Journal of Quantitative Criminology* 2014.

[55] Lindsay Miller and Jessica Toliver, *Implementing a Body-Worn Camera Program: Recommendations and Lessons Learned* (Washington, DC: Office of Community Oriented Policing Services, 2014), vii, http://ric-zai-inc.com/Publications/cops-p296-pub.pdf.

[56] Ibid., 1.

to gauge community sentiment regarding agency policies and practices. Social media can also help police identify the potential nature and location of gang and other criminal or disorderly activity such as spontaneous crowd gatherings.[57]

The Boston Police Department (BPD), for example, has long embraced both community policing and the use of social media. The department put its experience to good and highly visible use in April 2013 during the rapidly developing investigation that followed the deadly explosion of two bombs at the finish line of the Boston Marathon. The BPD successfully used Twitter to keep the public informed about the status of the investigation, to calm nerves and request assistance, to correct mistaken information reported by the press, and to ask for public restraint in the tweeting of information from police scanners. This demonstrated the level of trust and interaction that a department and a community can attain online.[58]

While technology is crucial to law enforcement, it is never a panacea. Its acquisition and use can have unintended consequences for both the organization and the community it serves, which may limit its potential. Thus, agencies need clearly defined policies related to implementation of technology, and must pay close attention to community concerns about its use.

3.1 RECOMMENDATION: The U.S. Department of Justice, in consultation with the law enforcement field, should broaden the efforts of the National Institute of Justice to establish national standards for the research and development of new technology. These standards should also address compatibility and interoperability needs both within law enforcement agencies and across agencies and jurisdictions and maintain civil and human rights protections.

The lack of consistent standards leads to a constantly spiraling increase in technology costs. Law enforcement often has to invest in new layers of technology to enable their systems to operate with different systems and sometimes must also make expensive modifications or additions to legacy systems to support interoperability with newer technology. And these costs do not include the additional funds needed for training. Agencies are often unprepared for the unintended consequences that may accompany the acquisition of new technologies. Implementation of new technologies can cause disruptions to daily routines, lack of buy-in, and lack of understanding of the purpose and appropriate uses of the technologies. It also often raises questions regarding how the new technologies will impact the officer's expectations, discretion, decision making, and accountability.[59]

---

[57] Police Executive Research Forum, *Social Media and Tactical Considerations for Law Enforcement* (Washington, DC: Office of Community Oriented Policing Services, 2013), http://ric-zai-inc.com/Publications/cops-p261-pub.pdf.

[58] Edward F. Davis III, Alejandro A. Alves, and David Alan Sklansky, "Social Media and Police Leadership: Lessons from Boston," *New Perspectives in Policing* (Washington, DC: National Institute of Justice, March 2014), http://www.hks.harvard.edu/content/download/67536/1242954/version/1/file/SocialMediaandPoliceLeadership-03-14.pdf.

[59] Koper et al., *Potential of Technology in Policing* (see note 52).

Inconsistent or non-existent standards also lead to isolated and fractured information systems that cannot effectively manage, store, analyze, or share their data with other systems. As a result, much information is lost or unavailable—which allows vital information to go unused and have no impact on crime reduction efforts. As one witness noted, the development of mature crime analysis and CompStat processes allows law enforcement to effectively develop policy and deploy resources for crime prevention, but there is a lack of uniformity in data collection throughout law enforcement, and only patchwork methods of near real-time information sharing exist.[60] These problems are especially critical in light of the threats from terrorism and cybercrime.

3.1.1 ACTION ITEM: The Federal Government should support the development and delivery of training to help law enforcement agencies learn, acquire, and implement technology tools and tactics that are consistent with the best practices of 21st century policing.

3.1.2 ACTION ITEM: As part of national standards, the issue of technology's impact on privacy concerns should be addressed in accordance with protections provided by constitutional law.

Though all constitutional guidelines must be maintained in the performance of law enforcement duties, the legal framework (warrants, etc.) should continue to protect law enforcement access to data obtained from cell phones, social media, GPS, and other sources, allowing officers to detect, prevent, or respond to crime.

3.1.3 ACTION ITEM: Law enforcement agencies should deploy smart technology that is designed to prevent the tampering with or manipulating of evidence in violation of policy.

3.2 RECOMMENDATION: The implementation of appropriate technology by law enforcement agencies should be designed considering local needs and aligned with national standards.

While standards should be created for development and research of technology at the national level, implementation of developed technologies should remain a local decision to address the needs and resources of the community.

In addition to the expense of acquiring technology, implementation and training also requires funds, as well as time, personnel, and physical capacity. A case in point is the Phoenix Police Department's adoption of BWCs mentioned by witness Michael White, who said that the real costs came on the back end for managing the vast amount of data generated by the cameras. He quoted the Chief of the Phoenix Police Department as saying that it would cost their department $3.5 million to not only outfit all of their officers with the cameras but also successfully manage the program.

3.2.1 ACTION ITEM: Law enforcement agencies should encourage public engagement and collaboration, including the use of community advisory bodies, when developing a policy for the use of a new technology.

[60] Listening Session on Technology and Social Media (oral testimony of Elliot Cohen, Maryland State Police, for the President's Task Force on 21st Century Policing, Cincinnati, OH, January 31, 2015).

Local residents will be more accepting of and respond more positively to technology when they have been informed of new developments and their input has been encouraged. How police use technology and how they share that information with the public is critical. Task force witness Jim Bueermann, president of the Police Foundation, addressed this issue, noting that concerns about BWCs include potential compromises to the privacy of both officers and citizens, who are reluctant to speak to police if they think they are being recorded. And as the task force co-chair, Charles Ramsey, noted, "Just having the conversation can increase trust and legitimacy and help departments make better decisions."

3.2.2 ACTION ITEM: Law enforcement agencies should include an evaluation or assessment process to gauge the effectiveness of any new technology, soliciting input from all levels of the agency, from line officer to leadership, as well as assessment from members of the community.[61]

Witnesses suggested that law enforcement agencies create an advisory group when adopting a new technology.[62] Ideally, it would include line officers, union representatives, and members from other departmental units, such as research and planning, technology, and internal affairs. External stakeholders, such as representatives from the prosecutor's office, the defense bar, advocacy groups, and citizens should also be included, giving each group the opportunity to ask questions, express their concerns, and offer suggestions on policy and training.

3.2.3. ACTION ITEM: Law enforcement agencies should adopt the use of new technologies that will help them better serve people with special needs or disabilities.

3.3 RECOMMENDATION: The U.S. Department of Justice should develop best practices that can be adopted by state legislative bodies to govern the acquisition, use, retention, and dissemination of auditory, visual, and biometric data by law enforcement.

These model policies and practices should at minimum address technology usage and data and evidence acquisition and retention, as well as privacy issues, accountability and discipline. They must also consider the impact of data collection and use on public trust and police legitimacy.

3.3.1 ACTION ITEM: As part of the process for developing best practices, the U.S. Department of Justice should consult with civil rights and civil liberties organizations, as well as law enforcement research groups and other experts, concerning the constitutional issues that can arise as a result of the use of new technologies.

---

[61] Sharon Stolting, Shawn Barrett, and David Kurz, Best Practices Guide for Acquisition of New Technology (Alexandria, VA: International Association of Chiefs of Police, n.d.), http://www.theiacp.org/portals/0/pdfs/BP-NewTechnology.pdf.

[62] Listening Session on Technology and Social Media: Body Cameras—Research and Legal Considerations (oral testimony of Michael White, professor, Arizona State University, for the President's Task Force on 21st Century Policing, Cincinnati, OH, January 31, 2015).

The U.S. Department of Justice should create toolkits for the most effective and constitutional use of multiple forms of innovative technology that will provide state, local, and tribal law enforcement agencies with a one-stop clearinghouse of information and resources.

3.3.3. ACTION ITEM: Law enforcement agencies should review and consider the Bureau of Justice Assistance's (BJA) Body Worn Camera Toolkit to assist in implementing BWCs.

A Body-Worn Camera Expert Panel of law enforcement leaders, recognized practitioners, national policy leaders, and community advocates convened a two-day workshop in February, 2015 to develop a toolkit and provide guidance and model policy for law enforcement agencies implementing BWC programs. Subject matter experts contributed ideas and content for the proposed toolkit while a panel composed of privacy and victim advocates contributed ideas and content for the toolkit to broaden input and ensure transparency.

3.4 RECOMMENDATION: Federal, state, local, and tribal legislative bodies should be encouraged to update public record laws.

The quickly evolving nature of new technologies that collect video, audio, information, and biometric data on members of the community can cause unforeseen consequences. Public record laws, which allow public access to information held by government agencies, including law enforcement, should be modified to protect the privacy of the individuals whose records they hold and to maintain the trust of the community.

Issues such as the accessibility of video captured through dashboard or body-worn cameras are especially complex. So too are the officer use of force events that will be captured by video camera systems and then broadcast by local media outlets. Use of force, even when lawful and appropriate, can negatively influence public perception and trust of police. Sean Smoot, task force member, addressed this by recalling the shooting of a Flagstaff, Arizona, police officer whose death was recorded by his BWC. Responding to public record requests by local media, the police department released the graphic footage, which was then shown on local TV and also on YouTube.[63] This illustration also raises questions concerning the recording of police interactions with minors and the appropriateness of releasing those videos for public view given their inability to give informed consent for distribution.

---

[63] Listening Session on Technology and Social Media (Sean Smoot, task force member, for the President's Task Force on 21st Century Policing, Cincinnati, OH, January 31, 2015).

3.5 RECOMMENDATION: Law enforcement agencies should adopt model policies and best practices for technology-based community engagement that increases community trust and access.

These policies and practices should at a minimum increase transparency and accessibility, provide access to information (crime statistics, current calls for service), allow for public posting of policy and procedures, and enable access and usage for persons with disabilities. They should also address issues surrounding the use of new and social media, encouraging the use of social media as a means of community interaction and relationship building, which can result in stronger law enforcement. As witness Elliot Cohen noted,

> We have seen social media support policing efforts in gathering intelligence during active assailant incidents: the Columbia Mall shooting and the Boston Marathon bombing. Social media allowed for a greater volume of information to be collected in an electronic format, both audibly and visually. [64]

Table 2. What types of social media does your agency currently use, and what types of social media do you plan to begin using within the next 2 to 5 years?

Photo REmoved Due to Copyright Restrictions

Note: PERF, with the support of the COPS Office and Target Corporation, disseminated a "Future of Policing" survey in 2012 to more than 500 police agencies; nearly 200 responded.
Source: Police Executive Research Forum, *Future Trends in Policing* (Washington, DC: Office of Community Oriented Policing Services, 2014), http://ric-zai-inc.com/Publications/cops-p282-pub.pdf.

---

[64] Listening Session on Technology and Social Media: Technology Policy (oral testimony of Elliot Cohen, lieutenant, Maryland State Police, for the President's Task Force on 21st Century Policing, Cincinnati, OH, January 31, 2015).

But to engage the community, social media must be responsive and current. Said Bill Schrier, "Regularly refresh the content to maintain and engage the audience, post content rapidly during incidents to dispel rumors, and use it for engagement, not just public information."[65] False or incorrect statements made via social media, mainstream media, and other means of technology deeply harm trust and legitimacy and can only be overcome with targeted and continuing community engagement and repeated positive interaction. Agencies need to unequivocally discourage falsities by underlining how harmful they are and how difficult they are to overcome.

Agencies should also develop policies and practices on social media use that consider individual officer expression, professional representation, truthful communication, and other concerns that can impact trust and legitimacy.

3.6 RECOMMENDATION: The Federal Government should support the development of new "less than lethal" technology to help control combative suspects.

The fatal shootings in Ferguson, Cleveland, and elsewhere have put the consequences of use of force front and center in the national news. Policies and procedures must change, but so should the weaponry. New technologies such as conductive energy devices (CED) have been developed and may be used and evaluated to decrease the number of fatal police interventions. Studies of CEDs have shown them to be effective at reducing both officer and civilian injuries. For example, in one study that compared seven law enforcement agencies that use CEDs with six agencies that do not, researchers found a 70 percent decrease in officer injuries and a 40 percent decrease in suspect injures.[66] But new technologies should still be subject to the appropriate use of force continuum restrictions. And Vincent Talucci made the point in his testimony that over-reliance on technological weapons can also be dangerous.[67]

---

[65] Listening Session on Technology and Social Media: Technology Policy (oral testimony of Bill Schrier, senior policy advisor, Office of the Chief Information Officer, State of Washington, for the President's Task Force on 21st Century Policing, Cincinnati, OH, January 31, 2015).

[66] Bruce Taylor et al., *Comparing Safety Outcomes in Police Use-Of-Force Cases for Law Enforcement Agencies That Have Deployed Conducted Energy Devices and A Matched Comparison Group That Have Not: A Quasi-Experimental Evaluation* (Washington, DC: Police Executive Research Forum, 2009), https://www.ncjrs.gov/pdffiles1/nij/grants/237965.pdf; John M. MacDonald, Robert J. Kaminski, and Michael R. Smith, "The Effect of Less-Lethal Weapons on Injuries in Police Use-of-Force Events," *American Journal of Public Health* 99, no. 12 (2009) 2268–2274, http://www.ncbi.nlm.nih.gov/pmc/articles/PMC2775771/pdf/2268.pdf; Bruce G. Taylor and Daniel J. Woods, "Injuries to Officers and Suspects in Police Use-of-Force Cases: A Quasi-Experimental Evaluation," *Police Quarterly* 13, no. 3 (2010): 260–289, http://pqx.sagepub.com/content/13/3/260.full.pdf.

[67] Listening Session on Technology and Social Media (oral testimony of Vincent Talucci, International Association of Chiefs of Police, for the President's Task Force on 21st Century Policing, Cincinnati, OH, January 31, 2015).

3.6.1 ACTION ITEM: Relevant federal agencies, including the U.S. Departments of Defense and Justice, should expand their efforts to study the development and use of new less than lethal technologies and evaluate their impact on public safety, reducing lethal violence against citizens, Constitutionality, and officer safety.

3.7 RECOMMENDATION: The Federal Government should make the development and building of segregated radio spectrum and increased bandwidth by FirstNet for exclusive use by local, state, tribal, and federal public safety agencies a top priority.[68]

A national public safety broadband network which creates bandwidth for the exclusive use of law enforcement, the First Responder Network (FirstNet) is considered a game-changing public safety project, which would allow instantaneous communication in even the most remote areas whenever a disaster or incident occurs. It can also support many other technologies, including video transmission from BWCs.

---

[68] Listening Session on Technology and Social Media: Technology Policy (oral testimony of Bill Schrier, senior policy advisor, Office of the Chief Information Officer, State of Washington, for the President's Task Force on 21st Century Policing, Cincinnati, OH, January 31, 2015).

Pillar Four: Community Policing & Crime Reduction

Community policing is a philosophy that promotes organizational strategies that support the systematic use of partnerships and problem-solving techniques to proactively address the immediate conditions that give rise to public safety issues such as crime, social disorder, and fear of crime.[69]

Over the past few decades, rates of both violent and property crime have dropped dramatically across the United States.[70] However, some communities and segments of the population have not benefited from the decrease as much as others, and some not at all.[71] Though law enforcement must concentrate their efforts in these neighborhoods to maintain public safety, sometimes those specific efforts arouse resentment in the neighborhoods the police are striving to protect.

Police interventions must be implemented with strong policies and training in place, rooted in an understanding of procedural justice. Indeed, without that, police interventions can easily devolve into racial profiling, excessive use of force, and other practices which disregard civil rights, causing negative reactions from people living in already challenged communities.

Yet mutual trust and cooperation, two key elements of community policing, are vital to protecting residents of these communities from the crime that plagues them. By combining a focus on intervention and prevention through problem solving with building collaborative partnerships with schools, social services, and other stakeholders, community policing not only improves public safety but also enhances social connectivity and economic strength, which increases community resilience to crime. And, as noted by one speaker, it improves job satisfaction for line officers, too.

In his testimony to the task force, Camden County, New Jersey, Police Chief J. Scott Thomson noted that community policing starts on the street corner, with respectful interaction between a police officer and a local resident, a discussion that need not be related to a criminal matter.[72] In fact, it is important that not all interactions be based on emergency calls or crime investigations.

---

[69] *Community Policing Defined* (Washington, DC: Office of Community Oriented Policing Services, 2014), http://ric-zai-inc.com/Publications/cops-p157-pub.pdf.

[70] "Crime Statistics for 2013 Released: Decrease in Violent Crimes and Property Crimes," Federal Bureau of Investigation, last modified November 10, 2014, http://www.fbi.gov/news/stories/2014/november/crime-statistics-for-2013-released/crime-statistics-for-2013-released.

[71] Listening Session on Community Policing and Crime Reduction: Building Community Policing Organizations (oral testimony of Chris Magnus, chief, Richmond [CA] Police Department, for the President's Task Force on 21st Century Policing, Phoenix, AZ, February 13, 2015).

[72] Listening Session on Community Policing and Crime Reduction: Using Community Policing to Reduce Crime (oral testimony of J. Scott Thomson, chief, Camden County [NJ] Police Department, for the President's Task Force on 21st Century Policing, Phoenix, AZ, February 13, 2015).

Another aspect of community policing that was discussed in the listening session on this topic is the premise that officers enforce the law *with* the people not just *on* the people. In reflecting this belief, some commented on the negative results of zero tolerance policies, which mete out automatic and predetermined actions by officers regardless of extenuating circumstances.

Community policing requires the active building of positive relationships with members of the community—on an agency as well as on a personal basis. This can be done through assigning officers to geographic areas on a consistent basis, so that through the continuity of assignment they have the opportunity to know the members of the community. It can also be aided by the use of programs such as Eagle County, Colorado's Law Enforcement Immigrant Advisory Committee, which the police department formed with Catholic Charities to help the local immigrant community.[73] This type of policing also requires participation in community organizations, local meetings and public service activities.

To be most effective, community policing also requires collaborative partnerships with agencies beyond law enforcement, such as Philadelphia's successful Police Diversion Program described by Kevin Bethel, Deputy Commissioner of Patrol Operations in the Philadelphia Police Department in his testimony to the task force.[74] This partnership with the Philadelphia Department of Human Services, the school district, the District Attorney's office, Family Court, and other stakeholders significantly reduced the number of arrests of minority youths for minor offenses.

Problem solving, another key element of community policing, is critical to prevention. And problems must be solved in partnership with the community in order to effectively address chronic crime and disorder problems. As Office of Community Oriented Policing Services Director Ronald L. Davis has said, "We need to teach new recruits that law enforcement is more than just cuffing 'perps'—it's understanding why people do what they do."[75]

---

[73] Listening Session on Community Policing and Crime Reduction: Building Community Policing Organizations (oral testimony of Chris Magnus, chief, Richmond [CA] Police Department, for the President's Task Force on 21st Century Policing, Phoenix, AZ, February 13, 2015).

[74] Listening Session on Community Policing and Crime Reduction: Using Community Policing to Reduce Crime (oral testimony of Kevin Bethel, deputy police commissioner, Philadelphia Police Department, for the President's Task Force on 21st Century Policing, Phoenix, AZ, February 13, 2015).

[75] Faye Elkins, "Five COPS Office Directors Look Back and Think Forward at the 20th Anniversary Celebration," *Community Policing Dispatch* 8, no. 1 (January 12, 2014), http://cops.usdoj.gov/html/dispatch/01-2015/cops_office_20th_anniversary.asp.

In summary, law enforcement's obligation is not only to reduce crime but also to do so fairly while protecting the rights of citizens. Any prevention strategy that unintentionally violates civil rights, compromises police legitimacy, or undermines trust is counterproductive from both ethical and cost-benefit perspectives. Ignoring these considerations can have both financial costs (e.g., law suits) and social costs (e.g., loss of public support).

It must also be stressed that the absence of crime is not the final goal of law enforcement. Rather, it is the promotion and protection of public safety while respecting the dignity and rights of all. And public safety and well-being cannot be attained without the community's belief that their well-being is at the heart of all law enforcement activities. It is critical to help community members see police as allies rather than as an occupying force and to work in concert with other community stakeholders to create more economically and socially stable neighborhoods.

4.1 RECOMMENDATION: Law enforcement agencies should develop and adopt policies and strategies that reinforce the importance of community engagement in managing public safety.

Community policing is not just about the relationship between individual officers and individual neighborhood residents. It is also about the relationship between law enforcement leaders and leaders of key institutions in a community, such as churches, businesses, and schools, supporting the community's own process to define prevention and reach goals.

Law enforcement agencies cannot ensure the safety of communities alone but should seek to contribute to the strengthening of neighborhood capacity to prevent and reduce crime through informal social control. More than a century of research shows that informal social control is a much more powerful mechanism for crime control and reduction than is formal punishment. And perhaps the best evidence for the preventive power of informal social control may be the millions of unguarded opportunities to commit crime that are passed up each day.[76]

4.1.1 ACTION ITEM: Law enforcement agencies should consider adopting preferences for seeking "least harm" resolutions, such as diversion programs or warnings and citations in lieu of arrest for minor infractions.

4.2 RECOMMENDATION: Community policing should be infused throughout the culture and organizational structure of law enforcement agencies.

---

[76] Lawrence Cohen and Marcus Felson, "Social Change and Crime Rate Trends: A Routine Activities Approach," *American Sociological Review* 44 (August 1979): 588–607.

Community policing must be a way of doing business by an entire police force, not just a specialized unit of that force.[77] The task force heard testimony from Chief J. Scott Thomson of Camden County, New Jersey, who noted that

> Community policing cannot be a program, unit, strategy or tactic. It must be the core principle that lies at the foundation of a police department's culture. The only way to significantly reduce fear, crime, and disorder and then sustain these gains is to leverage the greatest force multiplier: the people of the community.[78]

This message was closely echoed by Chris Magnus, the police chief in Richmond, California. To build a more effective partnership with residents and transform culture within the police department as well as in the community, the Richmond police made sure that *all* officers, not just a select few, were doing community policing and neighborhood problem solving. Every officer is expected to get to know the residents, businesses, community groups, churches, and schools on their beat and work with them to identify and address public safety challenges, including quality of life issues such as blight. Officers remain in the same beat or district for several years or more—which builds familiarity and trust.[79]

Testimony from a number of witnesses also made clear that hiring, training, evaluating, and promoting officers based on their ability and track record in community engagement—not just traditional measures of policing such as arrests, tickets, or tactical skills—is an equally important component of the successful infusion of community policing throughout an organization.

4.2.1 ACTION ITEM: Law enforcement agencies should evaluate officers on their efforts to engage members of the community and the partnerships they build. Making this part of the performance evaluation process places an increased value on developing partnerships.

4.2.2 ACTION ITEM: Law enforcement agencies should evaluate their patrol deployment practices to allow sufficient time for patrol officers to participate in problem solving and community engagement activities.

4.2.3 ACTION ITEM: The U.S. Department of Justice and other public and private entities should support research into the factors that have led to dramatic successes in crime reduction in some communities through the infusion of non-discriminatory policing and to determine replicable factors that could be used to guide law enforcement agencies in other communities.

---

[77] Tracey Meares, "Praying for Community Policing," *California Law Review* 90 (2002): 1593–1634, http://digitalcommons.law.yale.edu/fss_papers/518/.

[78] Listening Session on Community Policing and Crime Reduction: Using Community Policing to Reduce Crime (oral testimony of J. Scott Thomson, chief, Camden County [NJ] Police Department, for the President's Task Force on 21st Century Policing, Phoenix, AZ, February 13, 2015).

[79] Listening Session on Community Policing and Crime Reduction: Building Community Policing Organizations (oral testimony of Chris Magnus, chief, Richmond [CA] Police Department, for the President's Task Force on 21st Century Policing, Phoenix, AZ, February 13, 2015).

4.3 RECOMMENDATION: Law enforcement agencies should engage in multidisciplinary, community team approaches for planning, implementing, and responding to crisis situations with complex causal factors.

Collaborative approaches that engage professionals from across systems have emerged as model practices for addressing community problems that are not resolvable by the police alone. These team approaches call upon law enforcement agencies, service providers, and community support networks to work together to provide the right resources for the situation and foster sustainable change. Multiple witnesses before the task force spoke of departments who coordinate mental health response teams that include mental health professionals, social workers, crisis counselors, and other professionals making decisions alongside the police regarding planning, implementing, and responding to mental health crisis situations. But this model is applicable to a number of community problems that regularly involve a police response including homelessness, substance abuse, domestic violence, human trafficking, and child abuse. Ultimately, the idea is for officers to be trained and equipped to make use of existing community resources in the diffusion of crisis situations.

4.3.1 ACTION ITEM: The U.S. Department of Justice should collaborate with others to develop and disseminate baseline models of this crisis intervention team approach that can be adapted to local contexts.

4.3.3 ACTION ITEM: Communities should look to involve peer support counselors as part of multidisciplinary teams when appropriate. Persons who have experienced the same trauma can provide both insight to the first responders and immediate support to individuals in crisis.

4.3.4 ACTION ITEM: Communities should be encouraged to evaluate the efficacy of these crisis intervention team approaches and hold agency leaders accountable for outcomes.

4.4 RECOMMENDATION: Communities should support a culture and practice of policing that reflects the values of protection and promotion of the dignity of all, especially the most vulnerable.

The task force heard many different ways of describing a positive culture of policing. David Kennedy suggested there could be a Hippocratic Oath for Policing: First, Do No Harm.[80] Law enforcement officers' goal should be to avoid use of force if at all possible, even when it is allowed by law and by policy. Terms such as *fair and impartial policing, rightful policing, Constitutional policing, neighborhood policing, procedural justice,* and *implicit bias training* all address changing the culture of policing. Respectful language; thoughtful and intentional dialogue about the perception and reality of profiling and the mass incarceration of minorities; and consistent involvement, both formal and informal, in community events all help ensure that relationships of trust between police and community will be built. The vision of policing in the 21st century should be that of officers as guardians of human and constitutional rights.

---

[80] Listening Session on Community Policing and Crime Reduction: Using Community Policing to Reduce Crime (oral testimony of David Kennedy, professor, John Jay College of Criminal Justice, for the President's Task Force on 21st Century Policing, Phoenix, AZ, February 13, 2015).

4.4.1 ACTION ITEM: Because offensive or harsh language can escalate a minor situation, law enforcement agencies should underscore the importance of language used and adopt policies directing officers to speak to individuals with respect.

4.4.1 ACTION ITEM: Law enforcement agencies should develop programs that create opportunities for patrol officers to regularly interact with neighborhood residents, faith leaders, and business leaders.

4.5 RECOMMENDATION: Community policing emphasizes working with neighborhood residents to co-produce public safety. Law enforcement agencies should work with community residents to identify problems and collaborate on implementing solutions that produce meaningful results for the community.

As Delores Jones Brown testified, "Neighborhood policing provides an opportunity for police departments to do things with residents in the co-production of public safety rather than doing things to or for them."[81] Community policing is not just about the behavior and tactics of police; it is also about the civic engagement and capacity of communities to improve their own neighborhoods, their quality of life, and their sense of safety and well-being. Members of communities are key partners in creating public safety, so communities and police need mechanisms to engage with each other in consistent and meaningful ways. One model for formalizing this engagement is through a civilian governance system such as is found in Los Angeles. As Chief Charles Beck explained in testimony to the task force,

> The Los Angeles Police Department is formally governed by the Board of Police Commissioners, a five-person civilian body with each member appointed by the mayor. The Commission has formal authority to hire the Chief of Police, to set broad policy for the department, and to hold the LAPD and its chief accountable to the people.[82]

Community policing, therefore, is concerned with changing the way in which citizens respond to police in more constructive and proactive ways. If officers feel unsafe and threatened, their ability to operate in an open and shared dialogue with community is inhibited. On the other hand, the police have the responsibility to understand the culture, history, and quality of life issues of the entire community— youth, elders, faith communities, special populations—and to educate the community, including its children, on the role and function of police and ways the community can protect itself, be part of solving problems, and prevent crime. Community and police jointly share the responsibility for civil dialogue and interaction.

---

[81] Listening Session on Community Policing and Crime Reduction: Community Policing and Crime Prevention Research (oral testimony of Delores Jones Brown, professor, Department of Law, Police Science & Criminal Justice Administration, John Jay College of Criminal Justice, for the President's Task Force on 21st Century Policing, Phoenix, AZ, February 13, 2015).

[82] Listening Session on Policy and Oversight: Civilian Oversight (oral testimony of Charles Beck, chief, Los Angeles Police Department, for the President's Task Force on 21st Century Policing, Cincinnati, OH, January 30, 2015).

4.5.1 ACTION ITEM: Law enforcement agencies should schedule regular forums and meetings where all community members can interact with police and help influence programs and policy.

4.5.2 ACTION ITEM: Law enforcement agencies should engage youth and communities in joint training with law enforcement, citizen academies, ride-alongs, problem solving teams, community action teams, and quality of life teams.

4.5.3. ACTION ITEM: Law enforcement agencies should establish formal community/citizen advisory committees to assist in developing crime prevention strategies and agency policies as well as provide input on policing issues.

Larger agencies should establish multiple committees to ensure they inform all levels of the organization. The makeup of these committees should reflect the demographics of the community or neighborhood being served.

4.5.4 ACTION ITEM: Law enforcement agencies should adopt community policing strategies that support and work in concert with economic development efforts within communities.

As several witnesses, including Bill Geller, testified, public safety and the economic health of communities go hand in hand.[83] It is therefore important for agencies to work with local, state, and federal partners on projects devoted to enhancing the economic health of the communities in which departments are located.

4.6 RECOMMENDATION: Communities should adopt policies and programs that address the needs of children and youth most at risk for crime or violence and reduce aggressive law enforcement tactics that stigmatize youth and marginalize their participation in schools and communities.

The past decade has seen an explosion of knowledge about adolescent development and the neurological underpinnings of adolescent behavior. Much has also been learned about the pathways by which adolescents become delinquent, the effectiveness of prevention and treatment programs, and the long-term effects of transferring youths to the adult system and confining them in harsh conditions. These findings have raised doubts about a series of policies and practices of "zero tolerance" that have contributed to increasing the school-to-prison pipeline by criminalizing the behaviors of children as young as kindergarten age. Noncriminal offenses can escalate to criminal charges when officers are not trained in child and adolescent development and are unable to recognize and manage a child's emotional, intellectual, and physical development issues. School district policies and practices that push students out of schools and into the juvenile justice system cause great harm and do no good.

---

[83] Listening Session on Community Policing and Crime Reduction: Community Policing and Crime Prevention Research (oral testimony of Bill Geller, director, Geller & Associates, for the President's Task Force on 21st Century Policing, Phoenix, AZ, February 13, 2015).

One witness told the task force a stunning story about what happened to him one day when he was a high school freshman:

> As I walked down the hall, one of the police officers employed in the school noticed I did not have my identification badge with me. Before I could explain why I did not have my badge, I was escorted to the office and suspended for an entire week. I had to leave the school premises immediately. Walking to the bus stop, a different police officer pulled me over and demanded to know why I was not in school. As I tried to explain, I was thrown into the back of the police car. They drove back to my school to see if I was telling the truth, and I was left waiting in the car for over two hours. When they came back, they told me I was in fact suspended, but because the school did not provide me with the proper forms, my guardian and I both had to pay tickets for me being off of school property. The tickets together were 600 dollars, and I had a court date for each one. Was forgetting my ID worth missing school? Me being kicked out of school did not solve or help anything. I was at home alone watching Jerry Springer, doing nothing.[84]

4.6.1 ACTION ITEM: Education and criminal justice agencies at all levels of government should work together to reform policies and procedures that push children into the juvenile justice system.[85]

4.6.2 ACTION ITEM: In order to keep youth in school and to keep them from criminal and violent behavior, law enforcement agencies should work with schools to encourage the creation of alternatives to student suspensions and expulsion through restorative justice, diversion, counseling, and family interventions.

4.6.3 ACTION ITEM: Law enforcement agencies should work with schools to encourage the use of alternative strategies that involve youth in decision making, such as restorative justice, youth courts, and peer interventions.

The Federal Government could incentivize schools to adopt this practice by tying federal funding to schools implementing restorative justice practices.

4.6.4 ACTION ITEM: Law enforcement agencies should work with schools to adopt an instructional approach to discipline that uses interventions or disciplinary consequences to help students develop new behavior skills and positive strategies to avoid conflict, redirect energy, and refocus on learning.

---

[84] Listening Session on Community Policing and Crime Prevention (oral testimony of Michael Reynolds for the President's Task Force on 21st Century Policing, Phoenix, AZ, February 13, 2015).

[85] For more information about such policies and procedures, see the U.S. Department of Justice's Civil Rights Division and U.S. Department of Education's Office for Civil Rights, "Joint 'Dear Colleague' Letter," last updated February 4, 2014, http://www2.ed.gov/about/offices/list/ocr/letters/colleague-201401-title-vi.html.

4.6.5 ACTION ITEM: Law enforcement agencies should work with schools to develop and monitor school discipline policies with input and collaboration from school personnel, students, families, and community members. These policies should prohibit the use of corporal punishment and electronic control devices.

4.6.6 ACTION ITEM: Law enforcement agencies should work with schools to create a continuum of developmentally appropriate and proportional consequences for addressing ongoing and escalating student misbehavior after all appropriate interventions have been attempted.

4.6.7 ACTION ITEM: Law enforcement agencies should work with communities to play a role in programs and procedures to reintegrate juveniles back into their communities as they leave the juvenile justice system.

Although this recommendation—and therefore its action items—specifically focuses on juveniles, this task force believes that law enforcement agencies should also work with communities to play a role in re-entry programs for adults leaving prisons and jails.

4.6.8 ACTION ITEM: Law enforcement agencies and schools should establish memoranda of agreement for the placement of School Resource Officers that limit police involvement in student discipline.

Such agreements could include provisions for special training for School Resource Officers to help them better understand and deal with issues involving youth.

4.6.9 ACTION ITEM: The Federal Government should assess and evaluate zero tolerance strategies and examine the role of reasonable discretion when dealing with adolescents in consideration of their stages of maturation or development.

4.7 RECOMMENDATION: Communities need to affirm and recognize the voices of youth in community decision making, facilitate youth-led research and problem solving, and develop and fund youth leadership training and life skills through positive youth/police collaboration and interactions.

Youth face unique challenges when encountering the criminal justice system. Law enforcement contacts for apparent infractions create trauma and fear in children and disillusionment in youth, but proactive and positive youth interactions with police create the opportunity for coaching, mentoring, and diversion into constructive alternative activities. Moving testimony from a panel of young people allowed the task force members to hear how officers can lead youth out of the conditions that keep them in the juvenile justice system and into self-awareness and self-help.

Phoenix native Jose Gonzales, 21, first went to jail at age nine and had a chaotic childhood; but in turning his life towards a productive and healthy future, he vividly remembers one officer who made a difference:

> Needless to say, I have had a fair amount of interaction with law enforcement in my youth. Some has been very positive. Like the time that a School Resource Officer got me involved in an after school club. Officer Bill D. helped me stop being a bad kid and assisted with after school activities. He sought me out to be a part of a club that included all sorts of youth—athletes, academics—and helped me gain confidence in reaching out to other social circles beyond my troubled community. The important idea I'd like to convey is that approach is everything.[86]

4.7.1 ACTION ITEM: Communities and law enforcement agencies should restore and build trust between youth and police by creating programs and projects for positive, consistent, and persistent interaction between youth and police.

4.7.2 ACTION ITEM: Communities should develop community- and school-based evidence-based programs that mitigate punitive and authoritarian solutions to teen problems.

---

[86] Listening Session on Community Policing and Crime Reduction: Youth and Law Enforcement (oral testimony of Jose Gonzales for the President's Task Force on 21st Century Policing, Phoenix, AZ, February 13, 2015).

Pillar Five: Training & Education

As our nation becomes more pluralistic and the scope of law enforcement's responsibilities expands, the need for more and better training has become critical. Today's line officers and leaders must meet a wide variety of challenges including international terrorism, evolving technologies, rising immigration, changing laws, new cultural mores, and a growing mental health crisis. All states, territories, and the District of Columbia should establish standards for hiring, training, and education.

The skills and knowledge required to effectively deal with these issues requires a higher level of education as well as extensive and ongoing training in specific disciplines. The task force discussed these needs in depth, making recommendations for basic recruit and in-service training, as well as leadership development in a wide variety of areas:

- Community policing and problem-solving principles
- Interpersonal and communication skills
- Bias awareness
- Scenario-based, situational decision making
- Crisis intervention
- Procedural justice and impartial policing
- Trauma and victim services
- Mental health issues
- Analytical research and technology
- Languages and cultural responsiveness

Many who spoke before the task force recommended that law enforcement partner with academic institutions; organizations such as the International Association of Chiefs of Police (IACP), the Major Cities Chiefs Association (MCCA), the National Organization of Black Law Enforcement Executives (NOBLE), and the Police Executive Research Forum (PERF); and other sources of appropriate training. Establishing fellowships and exchange programs with other agencies was also suggested.

Other witnesses spoke about the police education now offered by universities, noting that undergraduate criminal justice and criminology programs provide a serviceable foundation but that short courses of mixed quality and even some graduate university degree programs do not come close to addressing the needs of 21st-century law enforcement.

In addition to discussion of training programs and educational expectations, witnesses at the listening session made clear that approaches to recruitment, hiring, evaluation, and promotion are also essential to developing a more highly educated workforce with the character traits and social skills that enable effective policing and positive community relationships.

To build a police force capable of dealing with the complexity of the 21st century, it is imperative that agencies place value on both educational achievements and socialization skills when making hiring decisions. Hiring officers who reflect the community they serve is also important not only to external relations but also to increasing understanding within the agency. On the other hand, task force member Connie Rice described the best line officer she knew—White, but better at relating to the African-American community than his Black colleagues. Her recommendation was to look for the character traits that support fairness, compassion, and cultural sensitivity.[87]

The need for understanding, tolerance, and sensitivity to African Americans, Latinos, recent immigrants, Muslims, and the LGBTQ community was discussed at length at the listening session, with witnesses giving examples of unacceptable behavior in law enforcement's dealings with all of these groups. Participants also discussed the need to move towards practices that respect all members of the community equally and away from policing tactics that can unintentionally lead to excessive enforcement against minorities.

Witnesses noted that officers need to develop the skills and knowledge necessary in the fight against terrorism by gaining an understanding of the links between normal criminal activity and terrorism, for example. What is more, this training must be ongoing, as threats and procedures for combatting terrorism evolve.

The need for realistic, scenario based training to better manage interactions and minimize using force was discussed by a number of witnesses. Others focused more on content than delivery: Dennis Rosenbaum suggested putting procedural justice at the center of training, not on the fringes.[88] Ronal Serpas recommended training on the effects of violence not only on the community and individual victims but also on police officers themselves, noting that exposure to violence can make individuals more prone to violent behavior.[89] And witnesses Bruce Lipman and David Friedman both spoke about providing officers with historical perspectives of policing in order to provide context as to why some communities have negative feelings towards the police and improve understanding of the role of the police in a democratic society.[90]

Though today's law enforcement professionals are highly trained and highly skilled operationally, they must develop specialized knowledge and understanding that enable fair and procedurally just policing and allow them to meet a wide variety of new challenges and expectations. Tactical skills are

---

[87] Listening Session on Training and Education (Connie Rice, task force member, for the President's Task Force on 21st Century Policing, Phoenix, AZ, February 14, 2015).

[88] Listening Session on Community Policing and Crime Reduction: Community Policing and Crime Prevention Research (oral testimony of Dennis Rosenbaum, professor, University of Illinois at Chicago, for the President's Task Force on 21st Century Policing, Phoenix, AZ, February 13, 2015).

[89] Listening Session on Training and Education: Special Training on Building Trust (oral testimony of Ronal Serpas, advisory board member, Cure Violence Chicago, for the President's Task Force on 21st Century Policing, Phoenix, AZ, February 14, 2015).

[90] Listening Session on Training and Education: Special Training on Building Trust (oral testimony of David C. Friedman, director of National Law Enforcement Initiatives, Anti-Defamation League, for the President's Task Force on 21st Century Policing, Phoenix, AZ, February 14, 2015); Listening Session on Training and Education: Special Training on Building Trust (oral testimony of Bruce Lipman, Procedural Justice Training, for the President's Task Force on 21st Century Policing, Phoenix, AZ, February 14, 2015).

important, but attitude, tolerance, and interpersonal skills are equally so. And to be effective in an ever-changing world, training must continue throughout an officer's career.

The goal is not only effective, efficient policing but also procedural justice and fairness. Following are the task force's recommendations for implementing career-long education and training practices for law enforcement in the 21st century.

5.1 RECOMMENDATION: The Federal Government should support the development of partnerships with training facilities across the country to promote consistent standards for high quality training and establish training innovation hubs.

A starting point for changing the culture of policing is to change the culture of training academies. The designation of certain training academies as federally supported regional "training innovation hubs" could act as leverage points for changing training culture while taking into consideration regional variations. Federal funding would be a powerful incentive to these designated academies to conduct the necessary research to develop and implement the highest quality curricula focused on the needs of 21st century American policing, along with cutting edge delivery modalities.

5.1.1 ACTION ITEM: The training innovation hubs should develop replicable model programs that use adult-based learning and scenario based training in a training environment modeled less like boot camp. Through these programs the hubs would influence nationwide curricula, as well as instructional methodology.

5.1.2 ACTION ITEM: The training innovation hubs should establish partnerships with academic institutions to develop rigorous training practices, evaluation, and the development of curricula based on evidence-based practices.

5.1.3 ACTION ITEM: The Department of Justice should build a stronger relationship with the International Association of Directors of Law Enforcement (IADLEST) in order to leverage their network with state boards and commissions of Peace Officer Standards and Training (POST).

The POSTs are critical to the development and implementation of statewide training standards and the certification of instructors and training courses, as well as integral to facilitating communication, coordination, and influence with the more than 650 police academies across the nation. This relationship would also serve as a pipeline for disseminating information and creating discussion around best practices.

5.2 RECOMMENDATION: Law enforcement agencies should engage community members in the training process.

Not only can they make important contributions to the design and implementation of training that reflects the needs and character of their community but it is also important for police training to be as transparent as possible. This will result in both a better informed public and a better informed officer.

Where appropriate and through managed programs, the community would

- learn about and evaluate the existing training within departments;
- provide input into shaping that some training content and delivery;
- in some cases, participate in training alongside officers.

5.2.1 ACTION ITEM: The U.S. Department of Justice should conduct research to develop and disseminate a toolkit on how law enforcement agencies and training programs can integrate community members into this training process.

5.3 RECOMMENDATION: Law enforcement agencies should provide leadership training to all personnel throughout their careers.

Standards and programs need to be established for every level of leadership from the first line to middle management to executive leadership. If there is good leadership and procedural justice within the agency, the officers are more likely to behave according to those standards in the community. As Chief Edward Flynn of the Milwaukee Police Department noted, "Flexible, dynamic, insightful, ethical leaders are needed to develop the informal social control and social capital required for a civil society to flourish."[91] One example of leadership training is Leading Police Organizations, a program developed by the IACP and modeled after the West Point Leadership Program, which offers training for all levels of agency management in programs based on a behavioral science approach to leading people groups, change, and organizations, focusing on the concept of "every officer a leader."

5.3.1 ACTION ITEM: Recognizing that strong, capable leadership is required to create cultural transformation, the U.S. Department of Justice should invest in developing learning goals and model curricula/training for each level of leadership.

This training should focus on organizational procedural justice, community policing, police accountability, teaching, coaching, mentoring, and communicating with the media and the public. Chief Kim Jacobs noted this in her testimony discussing current issues with training on reviewing investigations of police actions and prepare comprehensive reports for all stakeholders, including the media and citizens.[92] These standards should also influence requirements for promotion and continuing/ongoing education should also be required to maintain leadership positions.

5.3.2 ACTION ITEM: The Federal Government should encourage and support partnerships between law enforcement and academic institutions to support a culture that values ongoing education and the integration of current research into the development of training, policies, and practices.

---

[91] Listening Session on Training and Education (oral testimony of Edward Flynn, chief, Milwaukee Police Department, for the President's Task Force on 21st Century Policing, Phoenix, AZ, February 14, 2015).

[92] Listening Session on Training and Education (oral testimony of Kim Jacobs, chief, Columbus [OH] Division of Police, for the President's Task Force on 21st Century Policing, Phoenix, AZ, February 14, 2015).

5.3.3 ACTION ITEM: The U.S. Department of Justice should support and encourage cross-discipline leadership training.

This can be within the criminal justice system but also across governments, non-profits, and the private sector, including social services, legal aid, businesses, community corrections, education, the courts, mental health organizations, civic and religious organizations, and others. When people come together from different disciplines and backgrounds, there is a cross-fertilization of ideas that often leads to better solutions. Furthermore, by interacting with a more diverse group of professionals, police can establish a valuable network of contacts whose knowledge and skills differ from but complement their own. This opportunity does exist for front-line staff on a variety specialty topics but also needs to happen at decision/policy maker levels. For example, the National Alliance for Drug Endangered Children is an especially appropriate model for the value of cross-discipline training. Their written testimony to the task force explains how their training approach focuses on the formation of community partnerships that engage law enforcement and professionals from multiple disciplines to collaboratively identify and protect drug endangered children and their families.[93]

5.4 RECOMMENDATION: The U.S. Department of Justice should develop, in partnership with institutions of higher education, a national postgraduate institute of policing for senior executives with a standardized curriculum preparing them to lead agencies in the 21st century.

To advance American law enforcement, we must advance its leadership. To that end, the task force recommends the establishment of a top quality graduate institute of policing to provide ongoing leadership training, education, and research programs which will enhance the quality of law enforcement culture, knowledge, skills, practices and policies. Modeled after the Naval Postgraduate School in Monterey, California, this institute will be staffed with subject matter experts and instructors drawn from the nation's top educational institutions, who will focus on the real world problems that challenge today's and tomorrow's law enforcement, teaching practical skills and providing the most current information for improving policing services throughout the nation. This institute could even, as witness Lawrence Sherman proposed, "admit qualified applicants to a three-month residential course for potential police executives, concluding in an assessment center and examination that would certify qualified graduates to serve as chief police executives anywhere in the United States."[94]

---

[93] Listening Session on Training and Education (written testimony of the National Alliance for Drug Endangered Children for the President's Task Force on 21st Century Policing, Phoenix, AZ, February 14, 2015).

[94] Listening Session on The Future of Community Policing (oral testimony of Lawrence Sherman, Wolfson Professor of Criminology, University of Cambridge, and Distinguished University Professor, University of Maryland, for the President's Task Force on 21st Century Policing, Washington, DC, February 24, 2015).

The Office of Community Oriented Policing Services (COPS Office) and the Office of Justice Programs (OJP) should work with the law enforcement professional organizations to encourage modification of their curricula—for example, the Senior Management Institute for Police run by PERF and the Police Executive Leadership Institute managed by the Major Cities Chiefs Association.

Crisis intervention training (CIT) was developed in Memphis, Tennessee, in 1988 and has been shown to improve police ability to recognize symptoms of a mental health crisis, enhance their confidence in addressing such an emergency, and reduce inaccurate beliefs about mental illness.[96] It has been found that after completing CIT orientation, officers felt encouraged to interact with people suffering a mental health crisis and to delay their "rush to resolution."[97] Dr. Randolph Dupont, Chair of the Department of Criminology and Criminal Justice at the University of Memphis, spoke to the task force about the effectiveness of the Memphis Crisis Intervention Team (CIT), which stresses verbal intervention and other de-escalation techniques.

Noting that empathy training is an important component, Dr. Dupont said the Memphis CIT includes personal interaction between officers and individuals with mental health problems. Officers who had contact with these individuals felt more comfortable with them, and hospital mental health staff who participated with the officers had more positive views of law enforcement. CIT also provides a unique opportunity to develop cross-disciplinary training and partnerships.

---

[95] Listening Session on Training and Education: Supervisory, Leadership and Management Training (oral testimony of Kimberly Jacobs, chief, Columbus [OH] Division of Police, for the President's Task Force on 21st Century Policing, Phoenix, AZ, February 14, 2015); Listening Session on Training and Education (e-mail of Annie McKee, senior fellow, University of Pennsylvania, for the President's Task Force on 21st Century Policing, Phoenix, AZ, February 13–14, 2015); Listening Session on Training and Education (written testimony of Anthony Braga et al. for the President's Task Force on 21st Century Policing, Phoenix, AZ, February 13–14, 2015).

[96] Natalie Bonfine, Christian Ritter, and Mark R. Munetz, "Police Officer Perceptions of the Impact of Crisis Intervention Team (CIT) Programs," *International Journal of Law and Psychiatry* 37, no. 4 (July–August 2014): 341–350, doi:10.1016/j.ijlp.2014.02.004.

[97] Kelly E. Canada, Beth Angell, and Amy C. Watson, "Crisis Intervention Teams in Chicago: Successes on the Ground," *Journal of Police Crisis Negotiations* 10, no. 1–2 (2010), 86–100, doi:10.1080/15332581003792070.

5.7 RECOMMENDATION: POSTs should ensure that basic officer training includes lessons to improve social interaction as well as tactical skills.

These include topics such as critical thinking, social intelligence, implicit bias, fair and impartial policing, historical trauma, and other topics that address capacity to build trust and legitimacy in diverse communities and offer better skills for gaining compliance without the use of physical force. Basic recruit training must also include tactical and operations training on lethal and nonlethal use of force with an emphasis on de-escalation and tactical retreat skills.

5.8 RECOMMENDATION: POSTs should ensure that basic recruit and in-service officer training include curriculum on the disease of addiction.

It is important that officers be able to recognize the signs of addiction and respond accordingly when they are interacting with people who may be impaired as a result of their addiction. Science has demonstrated that addiction is a disease of the brain—a disease that can be prevented and treated and from which people can recover. The growing understanding of this science has led to a number of law enforcement agencies equipping officers with overdose-reversal drugs such as naloxone and the passage of legislation in many states that shield any person from civil and criminal liability if they administer naloxone.

The Obama Administration's drug policy reflects this understanding and emphasizes access to treatment over incarceration, pursuing "smart on crime" rather than "tough on crime" approaches to drug-related offenses, and support for early health interventions designed to break the cycle of drug use, crime, incarceration, and re-arrest.[98] And the relationship between incarceration and addiction is a significant one. A 2004 survey by the U.S. Department of Justice estimated that about 70 percent of state and 64 percent of federal prisoners regularly used drugs prior to incarceration.[99]

5.9 RECOMMENDATION: POSTs should ensure both basic recruit and in-service training incorporates content around recognizing and confronting implicit bias and cultural responsiveness.

As the nation becomes more diverse, it will become increasingly important that police officers be sensitive to and tolerant of differences. It is vital that law enforcement provide training that recognizes the unique needs and characteristics of minority communities, whether they are victims or witnesses of crimes, subjects of stops, or criminal suspects.

Keeshan Harley, a young Black man, testified that he estimates that he's been stopped and frisked more than 100 times and that he felt that the problem is not just a few individual bad apples, but the

---

[98] *A Drug Policy for the 21st Century, July 2014*, accessed February 27, 2015, http://www.whitehouse.gov/ondcp/drugpolicyreform.

[99] C. Mumola and J.C. Karberg, *Drug Use and Dependence, State and Federal Prisoners, 2004* (Washington, DC: U.S. Department of Justice, Office of Justice Programs, Bureau of Justice Statistics, 2007), http://www.bjs.gov/content/pub/pdf/dudsfp04.pdf.

systemic way policing treats certain communities—including low-income and young people, African Americans, LGBTQ people, the homeless, immigrants, and people with psychiatric disabilities. In so doing, police have produced communities of alienation and resentment.[100] He is arguably not alone in his opinions, given that research has shown that "of those involved in traffic and street stops, a smaller percentage of Blacks than Whites believed the police behaved properly during the stop."[101]

And in a 2012 Survey of LGBTQ/HIV contact with police, 25 percent of respondents with any recent police contact reported at least one type of misconduct or harassment, such as being accused of an offense they did not commit, verbal assault, being arrested for an offense they did not commit, sexual harassment, physical assault, or sexual assault.[102]

5.9.1 ACTION ITEM: Law enforcement agencies should implement ongoing, top down training for all officers in cultural diversity and related topics that can build trust and legitimacy in diverse communities. This should be accomplished with the assistance of advocacy groups that represent the viewpoints of communities that have traditionally had adversarial relationships with law enforcement.

5.9.2 ACTION ITEM: Law enforcement agencies should implement training for officers that covers policies for interactions with the LGBTQ population, including issues such as determining gender identity for arrest placement, the Muslim, Arab, and South Asian communities, and immigrant or non-English speaking groups, as well as reinforcing policies for the prevention of sexual misconduct and harassment.

5.10 RECOMMENDATION: POSTs should require both basic recruit and in-service training on policing in a democratic society.

Police officers are granted a great deal of authority, and it is therefore important that they receive training on the Constitutional basis of and the proper use of that power and authority. Particular focus should be placed on ensuring that Terry stops[103] are conducted within constitutional guidelines.

---

[100] Listening Session on Training and Education: Voices in the Community (oral testimony of Keeshan Harley, member, Communities United for Police Reform, for the President's Task Force on 21st Century Policing, Phoenix, AZ, February 14, 2015); see also Tracey L. Meares, "Programming Errors: Understanding the Constitutionality of Stop-and-Frisk as a Program, Not an Incident," University of Chicago Law Review (forthcoming).

[101] Lynn Langton, and Matthew Durose, *Police Behavior During Traffic and Street Stops, 2011, Special Report* (Washington, DC: U.S. Department of Justice Programs, Bureau of Justice Statistics, 2013), NCJ 242937.

[102] Listening Session on Policy and Oversight (written testimony of Lambda Legal for the President's Task Force on 21st Century Policing, Cincinnati, OH, January 30–31, 2015); Lambda Legal, *Protected and Served? Survey of LGBT/HIV Contact with Police, Courts, Prisons, and Security, 2014*, accessed February 28, 2015, http://www.lambdalegal.org/protected-and-served.

[103] *Terry* v. *Ohio*, 392 U.S. 1 (1968).

5.11 RECOMMENDATION: The Federal Government, as well as state and local agencies, should encourage and incentivize higher education for law enforcement officers.

While many believe that a higher level of required education could raise the quality of officer performance, law enforcement also benefits from a diverse range of officers who bring their cultures, languages, and life experiences to policing. Offering entry level opportunities to recruits without a college degree can be combined with the provision of means to obtain higher education throughout their career, thereby ensuring the benefits of a diverse staff with a well-educated police force and an active learning culture. Current student loan programs allow repayment based on income, and some already provide tuition debt forgiveness after 120 months of service in the government or nonprofit sector.

5.11.1 ACTION ITEM: The Federal Government should create a loan repayment and forgiveness incentive program specifically for policing.

This could be modeled on similar programs that already exist for government service and other fields or the reinstitution of funding for programs such as the 1960s and 70s Law Enforcement Education Program.

Table 3. College degree requirements for full-time instructors in state and local law enforcement training academies, by type of operating agency, 2006

Primary operating agency	Percentage of academies with a minimum educational requirement that included a college degree		
	Total	4-year degree	2-year degree
All types	19%	11%	8%
State Peace Officer Standards and Training	13%	13%	0%
State police	11%	7%	5%
Sheriff's office	2%	0%	2%
County police	5%	0%	5%
Municipal police	7%	4%	3%
College/university	35%	22%	13%
Multiagency	15%	2%	13%
Other types	8%	8%	0%

Source: Brian A. Reaves, "State and Local Law Enforcement Training Academies, 2006," *Special Report* (Washington, DC: Bureau of Justice Statistics, 2009), http://www.bjs.gov/content/pub/pdf/slleta06.pdf.

5.12 RECOMMENDATION: The Federal Government should support research into the development of technology that enhances scenario based training, social interaction skills, and enables the dissemination of interactive distance learning for law enforcement.

This will lead to new modalities that enhance the effectiveness of the learning experience, reduce instructional costs, and ensure the broad dissemination of training through platforms that do not require time away from agencies.

This would be especially helpful for smaller and more rural departments who cannot spare the time for their officers to participate in residential/in-person training programs. Present day technologies should also be employed more often—web based learning, behavior evaluations through body worn camera videos, software programs for independent learning, scenario-based instruction through videos, and other methods. This can also increase access to evidence based research and other sources of knowledge.

5.13 RECOMMENDATION: The U.S. Department of Justice should support the development and implementation of improved Field Training Officer programs.

This is critical in terms of changing officer culture. Field Training Officers impart the organizational culture to the newest members. The most common current program, known as the San Jose Model, is more than 40 years old and is not based on current research knowledge of adult learning modalities. In many ways it even conflicts with innovative training strategies that encourage problem-based learning and support organizational procedural justice.

5.13.1 ACTION ITEM: The U.S. Department of Justice should support the development of broad Field Training Program standards and training strategies that address changing police culture and organizational procedural justice issues that agencies can adopt and customize to local needs.

A potential model for this is the Police Training Officer program developed by the COPS Office in collaboration with PERF and the Reno (Nevada) Police Department. This problem based learning strategy used adult learning theory and problem solving tools to encourage new officers to think with a proactive mindset, enabling the identification of and solution to problems within their communities.

5.13.2 ACTION ITEM: The U.S. Department of Justice should provide funding to incentivize agencies to update their Field Training Programs in accordance with the new standards.

Pillar Six: Officer Wellness & Safety

Most law enforcement officers walk into risky situations and encounter tragedy on a regular basis. Some, such as the police who responded to the carnage of Sandy Hook Elementary School, witness horror that stays with them for the rest of their lives. Others are physically injured in carrying out their duties, sometimes needlessly, through mistakes made in high stress situations. The recent notable deaths of officers are stark reminders of the risk officers face. As a result, physical, mental, and emotional injuries plague many law enforcement agencies.

However, a large proportion of officer injuries and deaths are not the result of interaction with criminal offenders but the outcome of poor physical health due to poor nutrition, lack of exercise, sleep deprivation, and substance abuse. Yet these causes are often overlooked or given scant attention. Many other injuries and fatalities are the result of vehicular accidents.

The wellness and safety of law enforcement officers is critical not only to themselves, their colleagues, and their agencies but also to public safety. An officer whose capabilities, judgment, and behavior are adversely affected by poor physical or psychological health may not only be of little use to the community he or she serves but also a danger to it and to other officers. As task force member Tracey Meares observed, "Hurt people can hurt people."[104]

Commenting on the irony of law enforcement's lack of services and practices to support wellness and safety, Dr. Laurence Miller observed in his testimony that supervisors would not allow an officer to go on patrol with a deficiently maintained vehicle, an un-serviced duty weapon, or a malfunctioning radio—but pay little attention to the maintenance of what is all officers' most valuable resource: their brains.[105]

Officer suicide is also a problem: a national study using data of the National Occupational Mortality Surveillance found that police died from suicide 2.4 times as often as from homicides. And though depression resulting from traumatic experiences is often the cause, routine work and life stressors— serving hostile communities, working long shifts, lack of family or departmental support—are frequent motivators too.

In this pillar, the task force focused on many of the issues that impact and are impacted by officer wellness and safety, focusing on strategies in several areas: physical, mental, and emotional health; vehicular accidents; officer suicide; shootings and assaults; and the partnerships with social services, unions, and other organizations that can support solutions.

---

[104] Listening Session on Officer Safety and Wellness (comment of Tracey Meares, task force member, for the President's Task Force on 21st Century Policing, Washington, DC, February 23, 2015).

[105] Listening Session on Officer Safety and Wellness (oral testimony of Laurence Miller, psychologist, for the President's Task Force on 21st Century Policing, Washington, DC, February 23, 2015).

Physical injuries and death in the line of duty, while declining, are still too high. According to estimates of U.S. Bureau of Labor Statistics, more than 100,000 law enforcement professionals are injured in the line of duty each year. Many are the result of assaults, which underscores the need for body armor, but most are due to vehicular accidents.

To protect against assaults, Orange County (Florida) Sheriff Jerry Demings talked about immersing new officers in simulation training that realistically depicts what they are going to face in the real world. "I subscribe to an edict that there is no substitute for training and experience . . . deaths and injuries can be prevented through training that is both realistic and repetitive."[106]

But to design effective training first requires collecting substantially more information about the nature of injuries sustained by officers on the job. Dr. Alexander Eastman's testimony noted that the field of emergency medicine involves the analysis of vast amounts of data with regard to injuries in order to improve prevention as well as treatment.

> In order to make the job of policing more safe, a nationwide repository for [law enforcement officer] injuries sustained is desperately needed. A robust database of this nature, analyzed by medical providers and scientists involved in law enforcement, would allow for recommendations in tactics, training, equipment, medical care and even policies/procedures that are grounded in that interface between scientific evidence, best medical practice and sound policing.[107]

Poor nutrition and fitness are also serious threats, as is sleep deprivation. Many errors in judgment can be traced to fatigue, which also makes it harder to connect with people and control emotions. But administrative changes such as reducing work shifts can improve officer's feelings of well-being, and the implementation of mental health strategies can lessen the impact of the stress and trauma.

However, the most important factor to consider when discussing wellness and safety is the culture of law enforcement, which needs to be transformed. Support for wellness and safety should permeate all practices and be expressed through changes in procedures, requirements, attitudes, and behaviors. An agency work environment in which officers do not feel they are respected, supported, or treated fairly is one of the most common sources of stress. And research indicates that officers who feel respected by their supervisors are more likely to accept and voluntarily comply with departmental policies. This transformation should also overturn the tradition of silence on psychological problems, encouraging officers to seek help without concern about negative consequences.

---

[106] Listening Session on Officer Safety and Wellness: Officer Safety (oral testimony of Jerry Demings, sheriff, Orange County, FL, for the President's Task Force on 21st Century Policing, Washington, DC, February 23, 2015).

[107] Listening Session on Officer Safety and Wellness: Officer Safety (oral testimony of Dr. Alexander Eastman, lieutenant and deputy medical director, Dallas Police Department, for the President's Task Force on 21st Century Policing, Washington, DC, February 23, 2015).

Partnerships are another crucial element. An agency cannot successfully tackle these issues without partners such as industrial hygienists, chaplains, unions, and mental health providers. But no program can succeed without buy-in from agency leadership as well as the rank and file.

The "bulletproof cop" does not exist. The officers who protect us must also be protected—against incapacitating physical, mental, and emotional health problems as well as against the hazards of their job. Their wellness and safety are crucial for them, their colleagues, and their agencies, as well as the well-being of the communities they serve.

6.1 RECOMMENDATION: The U.S. Department of Justice should enhance and further promote its multi-faceted officer safety and wellness initiative.

As noted by all task force members during the listening session, wellness and safety supports public safety. Officers who are mentally or physical incapacitated cannot serve their communities adequately and can be a danger to the people they serve, to their fellow officers, and to themselves.

6.1.1 ACTION ITEM: Congress should establish and fund a national "Blue Alert" warning system.

Leveraging the current Amber Alert program used to locate abducted children, the Blue Alert would enlist the help of the public in finding suspects after a law enforcement officer is killed in the line of duty. Some similar state systems do exist, but there are large gaps; a national system is needed. In addition to aiding the apprehension of suspects, it would send a message about the importance of protecting law enforcement from undue harm.

6.1.2 ACTION ITEM: The U.S. Department of Justice, in partnership with the U.S. Department of Health and Human Services, should establish a task force to study mental health issues unique to officers and recommend tailored treatments.

Law enforcement officers are subject to more stress than the general population owing to the nature of their jobs. In addition to working with difficult—even hostile—individuals, responding to tragic events, and sometimes coming under fire themselves, they suffer from the effects of everyday stressors—the most acute of which often come from their agencies, because of confusing messages or non-supportive management; and their families, who do not fully understand the pressures the officers face on the job. And as witness Laurence Miller said, "When both work and family relations fray, the individual's coping abilities can be stretched to the limit, resulting in alcohol abuse, domestic violence, overaggressive policing, even suicide."[108]

---

[108] Listening Session on Officer Safety and Wellness (oral testimony of Laurence Miller, psychologist, for the President's Task Force on 21st Century Policing, Washington, DC, February 23, 2015).

To add to the problems of those suffering from psychological distress, law enforcement culture has not historically supported efforts to treat or even acknowledged mental health problems, which are usually seen as a sign of "weakness." The challenges and treatments of mental health issues should therefore be viewed within the context of law enforcement's unique culture and working environment.

This task force should also look to establish a national toll-free mental health hotline specifically for police officers. This would be a fast, easy, and confidential way for officers to get advice whenever they needed to; and because they would be anonymous, officers would be more likely to take advantage of this resource. Since nobody understands the challenges an officer faces like another officer, it should be peer driven—anonymously connecting callers to officers who are not in the same agency and who could refer the caller to professional help if needed. An advisory board should be formed to guide the creation of this hotline service.

6.1.3 ACTION ITEM: The Federal Government should support the continuing research into the efficacy of an annual mental health check for officers, as well as fitness, resilience, and nutrition.

Currently, most mental health checks are ordered as interventions for anger management or substance abuse and are ordered reactively after an incident. Mental health checks need to be more frequent to prevent problems. Because officers are exposed to a wide range of stressors on a continuous basis as part of their daily routines, mental and physical health check-ups should be conducted on an ongoing basis. Furthermore, officer nutrition and fitness issues change with time, varying widely from those of the new academy graduate to those of the veteran who has spent the last five years sitting in a squad car. Many health problems—notably cardiac issues—are cumulative.

6.1.4. ACTION ITEM: Pension plans should recognize fitness for duty examinations as definitive evidence of valid duty or non-duty related disability.

Officers who have been injured in the line of duty can exist in limbo, without pay, unable to work but also unable to get benefits because the "fitness for duty" examinations given by their agencies are not recognized as valid proof of disability. And since officers, as public servants, cannot receive social security, they can end up in a precarious financial state.

6.1.5 ACTION ITEM: Public Safety Officer Benefits (PSOB) should be provided to survivors of officers killed while working, regardless of whether the officer used safety equipment (seatbelt or anti-ballistic vest) or if officer death was the result of suicide attributed to a current diagnosis of duty-related mental illness, including but not limited to post-traumatic stress disorder (PTSD).

Families should not be penalized because an officer died in the line of duty but was not wearing a seat belt or body armor. Though these precautions are very important and strongly encouraged, there are occasions when officers can be more effective without them.[109]

A couple of situations were mentioned by task force member Sean Smoot, who described the efforts of an officer who took off his seat belt to tend to the injuries of a victim in the back of the car as his partner sped to the hospital. Another scenario he mentioned was the rescue of a drowning woman by an officer who shed his heavy body armor to go into the water. Charles Ramsey, task force co-chair, also noted that these types of situations could be further mitigated by the invention of seatbelts that officers could quickly release without getting tangled on their belts, badges, and radios, as well as body armor that is lighter and more comfortable.

6.2 RECOMMENDATION: Law enforcement agencies should promote safety and wellness at every level of the organization.

Safety and wellness issues affect all law enforcement professionals, regardless of their management status, duty, or tenure. Moreover, line officers are more likely to adopt procedures or change practices if they are advised to do so by managers who also model the behavior they encourage. According to witness David Orr, buy-in from the leaders as well as the rank and file is essential to the success of any program.[110]

6.2.1 ACTION ITEM: Though the Federal Government can support many of the programs and best practices identified by the U.S. Department of Justice initiative described in recommendation 6.1, the ultimate responsibility lies with each agency.

Though legislation and funding from the Federal Government is necessary in some cases, most of the policies, programs, and practices recommended by the task force can and should be implemented at the local level. It is understood, however, that there are no "one size fits all" solutions and that implementation will vary according to agency size, location, resources, and other factors.

6.3 RECOMMENDATION: The U.S. Department of Justice should encourage and assist departments in the implementation of scientifically supported shift lengths by law enforcement.

---

[109] Listening Session on Officer Safety and Wellness: Voices from the Field (oral testimony of William Johnson, executive director, National Association of Police Organizations, for the President's Task Force on 21st Century Policing, Washington, DC, February 23, 2015).

[110] Listening Session on Officer Safety and Wellness (oral testimony of David Orr, sergeant, Norwalk [CT] Police Department, to the President's Task Force on 21st Century Policing, Washington, DC, February 23, 2015).

It has been established by significant bodies of research that long shifts can not only cause fatigue, stress, and decreased ability to concentrate but also lead to other more serious consequences.[111] Fatigue and stress undermine not only the immune system but also the ability to work at full capacity, make decisions, and maintain emotional equilibrium. Though long shifts are understandable in the case of emergencies, as a standard practice they can lead to poor morale, poor job performance, irritability, and errors in judgment that can have serious, even deadly, consequences.

6.3.1 ACTION ITEM: The U.S. Department of Justice should fund additional research into the efficacy of limiting the total number of hours an officer should work within a 24–48 hour period, including special findings on the maximum number of hours an officer should work in a high risk or high stress environment (e.g., public demonstrations or emergency situations).

6.4 RECOMMENDATION: Every law enforcement officer should be provided with individual tactical first aid kits and training as well as anti-ballistic vests.

Task force witness Dr. Alexander Eastman, who is a trauma surgeon as well as a law enforcement professional, noted that tactical first aid kits would significantly reduce the loss of both officer and civilian lives due to blood loss. Already available to members of the military engaged in combat missions, these kits are designed to save lives by controlling hemorrhaging. They contain tourniquets, an Olaes modular bandage, and QuikClot gauze and would be provided along with training in hemorrhage control. Dr. Eastman estimated that the kits could cost less than $50 each and require about two hours of training, which could be provided through officers who have completed "train the trainer" programs.[112]

This would be a national adoption of the Hartford Consensus, which calls for agencies to adopt hemorrhage control as a core law enforcement skill and to integrate rescue/emergency medical services personnel into community-wide active shooter preparedness and training. These activities would complement the current "Save Our Own" law enforcement-based hemorrhage control programs.[113]

---

[111] Bryan Vila, *Tired Cops: The Importance of Managing Police Fatigue*, (Washington, DC: Police Executive Research Forum, 2000); Mora L. Fiedler, *Officer Safety and Wellness: An Overview of the Issues* (Washington, DC: Office of Community Oriented Policing Services, 2011), 4, http://cops.usdoj.gov/pdf/OSWG/e091120401-OSWGReport.pdf.

[112] Listening Session on Officer Safety and Wellness: Officer Safety (oral testimony of Dr. Alexander Eastman, lieutenant and deputy medical director, Dallas Police Department, for the President's Task Force on 21st Century Policing, Washington, DC, February 23, 2015).

[113] M. Jacobs Lenworth, Jr., "Joint Committee to Create a National Policy to Enhance Survivability from Mass Casualty Shooting Events: Hartford Consensus II," *Journal of the American College of Surgeons* 218, no. 3 (March 2014): 476–478.

To further reduce officer deaths, the task force also strongly recommends the provision of body armor to all officers with replacements when necessary.

6.4.1 ACTION ITEM: Congress should authorize funding for the distribution of law enforcement individual tactical first-aid kits.

6.4.2 ACTION ITEM: Congress should reauthorize and expand the Bulletproof Vest Partnership (BVP) program.

Created by statute in 1998, this program is a unique U.S. Department of Justice initiative designed to provide a critical resource to state and local law enforcement. Based on data collected and recorded by Bureau of Justice Assistance staff, in FY 2012 protective vests were directly attributed to saving the lives of at least 33 law enforcement and corrections officers.

6.5 RECOMMENDATION: The U.S. Department of Justice should expand efforts to collect and analyze data not only on officer deaths but also on injuries and "near misses."

Another recommendation mentioned by multiple witnesses is the establishment of a nationwide repository of data on law enforcement injuries, deaths, and near misses. Though the Federal Bureau of Investigation (FBI) does maintain a database of information pertinent to police procedures on officers killed in the line of duty, it does not contain the medical details that could be analyzed by medical providers and scientists to improve medical care, tactics, training, equipment, and procedures that would prevent or reduce injuries and save lives. The Police Foundation, with the support of a number of other law enforcement organizations, launched an online Law Enforcement Near Miss Reporting System in late 2014, but it is limited in its ability to systematically analyze national trends in this important data by its voluntary nature.[114]

6.6 RECOMMENDATION: Law enforcement agencies should adopt policies that require officers to wear seat belts and bullet-proof vests and provide training to raise awareness of the consequences of failure to do so.

According to task force witness Craig Floyd, traffic accidents have been the number one cause of officer fatalities in recent years, and nearly half of those officers were not wearing seat belts.[115] He suggests in-car cameras and seat belt sensors to encourage use along with aggressive safety campaigns. Some witnesses endorsed mandatory seat belt policies as well.

---

[114] Deborah L. Spence, "One on One with LEO Near Miss," *Community Policing Dispatch* 8, no. 2 (February 2015), http://cops.usdoj.gov/html/dispatch/02-2015/leo_near_miss.asp.

[115] Listening Session on Officer Safety and Wellness (oral testimony of Craig Floyd, National Law Enforcement Officer Memorial Foundation, for the President's Task Force on 21st Century Policing, Washington, DC, February 23, 2015).

The Prince George's County Arrive Alive Campaign initiated by task force witness Chief Mark Magraw to promote 100 percent seat belt usage relied on incentives and peer pressure for success. The message was, "it is not just about you, it is also about your family and your department."[116]

There were also many calls for mandatory requirements that all officers wear soft body armor any time they are going to be engaging in enforcement activities, uniformed or not. It was also suggested that law enforcement agencies be required to provide these for all commissioned personnel.

6.7 RECOMMENDATION: Congress should develop and enact peer review error management legislation.

The task force recommends that Congress enact legislation, similar to the Healthcare Quality Improvement Act of 1986,[117] that would support the development of an effective peer review error management system for law enforcement similar to what exists in medicine. A robust but nonpunitive peer review error management program—in which law enforcement officers could openly and frankly discuss their own or others' mistakes or near misses *without fear of legal repercussions*—would go a long way toward reducing injuries and fatalities by improving tactics, policies, and procedures. Protecting peer review error management findings from being used in legal discovery would enable the widespread adoption of this program by law enforcement.

The Near Miss anonymous reporting system developed by the Police Foundation in Washington, D.C. currently collects anonymous data that can be very helpful in learning from and preventing mistakes, fatalities, and injuries—but a program that enabled peer review of errors would provide even more valuable perspectives and solutions.

6.8 RECOMMENDATION: The U.S. Department of Transportation should provide technical assistance opportunities for departments to explore the use of vehicles equipped with vehicle collision prevention "smart car" technology that will reduce the number of accidents.

Given that the FBI's 2003 to 2012 Law Enforcement Officers Killed in Action report showed that 49 percent of officer fatalities were a result of vehicle-related accidents, the need for protective devices cannot be understated. New technologies such as vehicle prevention systems should be explored.

---

[116] Listening Session on Officer Safety and Wellness (oral testimony of Mark Magraw, chief, Prince Georges County [MD] Police Department, for the President's Task Force on 21st Century Policing, Washington, DC, February 23, 2015).

[117] The Health Care Quality Improvement Act of 1986 (HCQIA), 42 USC §11101 et seq., sets out standards for professional review actions. If a professional review body meets these standards, then neither the professional review body nor any person acting as a member or staff to the body will be liable in damages under most federal or state laws with respect to the action. For more information, see "Medical Peer Review," American Medical Association, accessed February 28, 2015, http://www.ama-assn.org/ama/pub/physician-resources/legal-topics/medical-peer-review.page.

Figure 2. Total fatalities from 1964–2014

Photo Removed Due to copyright Restrictions

Source: "126 Law Enforcement Fatalities Nationwide in 2014," *Preliminary 2014 Law Enforcement Officer Fatalities Report* (Washington, DC: National Law Enforcement Officers Memorial Fund, December 2014), http://www.nleomf.org/assets/pdfs/reports/Preliminary-2014-Officer-Fatalities-Report.pdf.

Implementation

The members of the President's Task Force on 21st Century Policing are convinced that these 59 concrete recommendations for research, action, and further study will bring long-term improvements to the ways in which law enforcement agencies interact with and bring positive change to their communities. But we also recognize that the Administration, through policies and practices already in place, can start right now to move forward on the bedrock recommendations in this report. Accordingly, we propose the following items for immediate action.

7.1 RECOMMENDATION: The President should direct all federal law enforcement agencies to review the recommendations made by the Task Force on 21st Century Policing and, to the extent practicable, to adopt those that can be implemented at the federal level.

7.2 RECOMMENDATION: The U.S. Department of Justice should explore public-private partnership opportunities, starting by convening a meeting with local, regional, and national foundations to discuss the proposals for reform described in this report and seeking their engagement and support in advancing implementation of these recommendations.

7.3 RECOMMENDATION: The U.S. Department of Justice should charge its Office of Community Oriented Policing Services (COPS Office) with assisting the law enforcement field in addressing current and future challenges.

For recommendation 7.3, the COPS Office should consider taking actions including but not limited to the following:

- Create a National Policing Practices and Accountability Division within the COPS Office.

- Establish national benchmarks and best practices for federal, state, local, and tribal police departments.

- Provide technical assistance and funding to national, state, local, and tribal accreditation bodies that evaluate policing practices.

- Recommend additional benchmarks and best practices for state training and standards boards.

- Provide technical assistance and funding to state training boards to help them meet national benchmarks and best practices in training methodologies and content.

- Prioritize grant funding to departments meeting benchmarks.

- Support departments through an expansion of the COPS Office Collaborative Reform Initiative.

- Collaborate with universities, the Office of Justice Programs and its bureaus (Bureau of Justice Assistance [BJA], Bureau of Justice Statistics [BJS], National Institute of Justice [NIJ], and Office of Juvenile Justice and Delinquency Prevention [OJJDP]), and others to review research and literature in order to inform law enforcement agencies about evidence-based practices and to identify areas of police operations where additional research is needed.

- Collaborate with the BJS to

  - establish a central repository for data concerning police use of force resulting in death, as well as in-custody deaths, and disseminate this data for use by both community and police;

  - provide local agencies with technical assistance and a template to conduct local citizen satisfaction surveys;

  - compile annual citizen satisfaction surveys based on the submission of voluntary local surveys, develop a national level survey as well as surveys for use by local agencies and by small geographic units, and develop questions to be added to the National Crime Victimization Survey relating to citizen satisfaction with police agencies and public trust.

- Collaborate with the BJS and others to develop a template of broader indicators of performance for police departments beyond crime rates alone that could comprise a Uniform Justice Report.

- Collaborate with the NIJ and the BJS to publish an annual report on the "State of Policing" in the United States.

- Provide support to national police leadership associations and national rank and file organizations to encourage them to implement task force recommendations.

- Work with the U.S. Department of Homeland Security to ensure that community policing tactics in state, local, and tribal law enforcement agencies are incorporated into their role in homeland security.

Appendix A. Public Listening Sessions & Witnesses

The President's Task Force on 21st Century Policing hosted multiple public listening sessions to gain broad input and expertise from stakeholders. The information collected in these meetings informed and advised the task force in developing its recommendations.

Listening Session 1: Building Trust & Legitimacy

Washington, D.C., January 13, 2015

Panel One: Subject Matter Experts

Jennifer Eberhardt, Associate Professor of Psychology, Stanford University

Charles Ogletree, Jesse Climenko Professor of Law, Harvard Law School

Tom Tyler, Macklin Fleming Professor of Law and Professor of Psychology, Yale Law School

Samuel Walker, Emeritus Professor of Criminal Justice, University of Nebraska Omaha

Panel Two: Community Representatives

Carmen Perez, Executive Director, The Gathering for Justice

Jim St. Germain, Co-Founder, Preparing Leaders of Tomorrow, Inc.

Jim Winkler, President and General Secretary, National Council of Churches of Christ in the USA

Panel Three: Law Enforcement Organizations

Richard Beary, President, International Association of Chiefs of Police

Chuck Canterbury, National President, Fraternal Order of Police

Andrew Peralta, National President, National Latino Peace Officers Association

Richard Stanek, Immediate Past President, Major County Sheriffs' Association

Panel Four: Civil Rights / Civil Liberties

Sherrilyn Ifill, President and Director-Counsel, National Association for the Advancement of Colored People Legal Defense and Educational Fund

Maria Teresa Kumar, President and CEO, Voto Latino

Laura Murphy, Director, Washington Legislative Office, American Civil Liberties Union

Vikrant Reddy, Senior Policy Analyst, Texas Public Policy Foundation Center for Effective Justice

Panel Five: Mayors

Kevin Johnson, Mayor, Sacramento

Michael Nutter, Mayor, Philadelphia

Stephanie Rawlings-Blake, Mayor, Baltimore

Listening Session 2: Policy & Oversight

Cincinnati, Ohio, January 30, 2015

Panel One: Use of Force Research and Policies

Geoffrey Alpert, Professor, University of South Carolina

Mick McHale, Vice President, National Association of Police Organizations

Harold Medlock, Chief, Fayetteville (North Carolina) Police Department

Rashad Robinson, Executive Director, Color of Change

Panel Two: Use of Force Investigations and Oversight

Sim Gill, District Attorney, Salt Lake County, Utah

Jay McDonald, President, Fraternal Order of Police of Ohio

Kirk Primas, Deputy Chief, Las Vegas Metropolitan Police Department

Chuck Wexler, Executive Director, Police Executive Research Forum

Panel Three: Civilian Oversight

Charlie Beck, Chief, Los Angeles Police Department

Brian Buchner, President, National Association for Civilian Oversight of Law Enforcement

Darius Charney, Senior Staff Attorney, Center for Constitutional Rights

Panel Four: Mass Demonstrations

Christina Brown, Member, Black Lives Matter: Cincinnati

Garry McCarthy, Superintendent, Chicago Police Department

Rodney Monroe, Chief, Charlotte-Mecklenburg (North Carolina) Police Department

Sean Whent, Chief, Oakland (California) Police Department

Panel Five: Law Enforcement Culture and Diversity

Malik Aziz, National Chairman, National Black Police Association

Hayley Gorenberg, Deputy Legal Director, Lambda Legal

Kathy Harrell, President, Fraternal Order of Police, Queen City Lodge #69, Cincinnati, Ohio

Barbara O'Connor, President, National Association of Women Law Enforcement Executives

Listening Session 3: Technology & Social Media

Cincinnati, Ohio, January 31, 2015

Panel One: Body Cameras—Research and Legal Considerations

Jim Bueermann, President, Police Foundation

Scott Greenwood, Attorney

Tracie Keesee, Co-Founder and Director of Research Partnerships, Center for Policing Equity

Bill Lewinski, Executive Director, Force Science Institute

Michael White, Professor, School of Criminology and Criminal Justice, Arizona State University

Panel Two: Body Cameras—Implementation

Johanna Miller, Advocacy Director, New York Civil Liberties Union

Ken Miller, Chief, Greenville (South Carolina) Police Department

Kenton Rainey, Chief, Bay Area Rapid Transit, San Francisco

Richard Van Houten, Sergeant, Fort Worth (Texas) Police Officers Association

Panel Three: Technology Policy

Eliot Cohen, Lieutenant, Maryland State Police

Madhu Grewal, Policy Counsel, The Constitution Project

Bill Schrier, Senior Policy Advisor, Office of the Chief Information Officer, State of Washington

Vincent Talucci, Executive Director / Chief Executive Officer, International Association of Chiefs of Police

Panel Four: Social Media, Community Digital Engagement and Collaboration

Hassan Aden, Director, Research and Programs, International Association of Chiefs of Police

DeRay McKesson, This is the Movement

Steve Spiker, Research and Technology Director, Urban Strategies Council

Lauri Stevens, Founder and Principal Consultant, LAwS Communications

Listening Session 4: Community Policing & Crime Reduction

Phoenix, Arizona, February 13, 2015

Panel One: Community Policing and Crime Prevention Research

Bill Geller, Director, Geller & Associates

Dr. Delores Jones-Brown, Professor, John Jay College of Criminal Justice, City University of New York

Dr. Dennis Rosenbaum, Professor, University of Illinois at Chicago

Dr. Wesley G. Skogan, Professor, Northwestern University

Panel Two: Building Community Policing Organizations

Anthony Batts, Police Commissioner, Baltimore Police Department

Jeffrey Blackwell, Chief, Cincinnati (Ohio) Police Department

Chris Magnus, Chief, Richmond (California) Police Department

Patrick Melvin, Chief, Salt River Police Department (Salt River Pima-Maricopa Indian Community)

Panel Three: Using Community Policing to Reduce Crime

Kevin Bethel, Deputy Police Commissioner, Philadelphia Police Department

Melissa Jones, Senior Program Officer, Boston's Local Initiatives Support Corporation

David Kennedy, Professor, John Jay College of Criminal Justice, City University of New York

J. Scott Thomson, Chief, Camden County (New Jersey) Police Department

George Turner, Chief, Atlanta Police Department

Panel Four: Using Community Policing to Restore Trust

Rev. Jeff Brown, Rebuilding Every City Around Peace

Dwayne Crawford, Executive Director, National Organization of Black Law Enforcement Executives

Justin Hansford, Assistant Professor of Law, Saint Louis University School of Law

Cecil Smith, Chief, Sanford (Florida) Police Department

Panel Five: Youth and Law Enforcement

Delilah Coleman, Member, Navajo Nation (Senior at Flagstaff High School)

Jose Gonzales, Alumnus, Foster Care and Crossover Youth

Jamecia Luckey, Youth Conference Committee Member, Cocoa (Florida) Police Athletic League

Nicholas Peart, Staff Member, The Brotherhood-Sister Sol (Class Member, *Floyd, et al.* v. *City of New York, et al.*)

Michael Reynolds, Co-President, Youth Power Movement

Listening Session 5: Training & Education

Phoenix, Arizona, February 14, 2015

Panel One: Basic Recruit Academy

Arlen Ciechanowski, President, International Association of Directors of Law Enforcement Standards and Training

William J. Johnson, Executive Director, National Association of Police Organizations

Benjamin B. Tucker, First Deputy Commissioner, New York City Police Department

Dr. Steven Winegar, Coordinator, Public Safety Leadership Development, Oregon Department of Public Safety Standards and Training

Panel Two: In-Service Training

Dr. Scott Decker, Professor, Arizona State University

Aaron Danielson, President, Public Safety Employee Association/AFSCME Local 803, Fairbanks, Alaska

Dr. Cheryl May, Director, Criminal Justice Institute and National Center for Rural Law Enforcement

John Ortolano, President, Arizona Fraternal Order of Police

Gary Schofield, Deputy Chief, Las Vegas Metropolitan Police Department

Panel Three: Supervisory, Leadership and Management Training

Edward Flynn, Chief, Milwaukee (Wisconsin) Police Department

Sandra Hutchens, Sheriff, Orange County (California) Sheriff's Department

Kimberly Jacobs, Chief, Columbus (Ohio) Division of Police

John Layton, Sheriff, Marion County (Indiana) Sheriff's Office

Dr. Ellen Scrivner, Executive Fellow, Police Foundation

Panel Four: Voices in the Community

Allie Bones, MSW, Chief Executive Officer, Arizona Coalition to End Sexual and Domestic Violence

Renaldo Fowler, Staff Advocate, Arizona Center for Disability Law

Keeshan Harley, Member, Communities United for Police Reform

Andrea Ritchie, Senior Policy Counsel, Streetwise and Safe

Linda Sarsour, Director, Arab American Association of New York

Panel Five: Special Training on Building Trust

Lt. Sandra Brown (retired), Principal Trainer, Fair and Impartial Policing

Dr. Randolph Dupont, Professor and Clinical Psychologist, University of Memphis

David C. Friedman, Director of National Law Enforcement Initiatives, Anti-Defamation League

Lt. Bruce Lipman (retired), Procedural Justice Training

Dr. Ronal Serpas, Advisory Board Member, Cure Violence Chicago

Listening Session 6: Officer Safety & Wellness

Washington, DC, February 23, 2015

Panel One: Officer Wellness

Dr. Laurence Miller, Clinical Psychologist

David Orr, Sergeant, Norwalk (Connecticut) Police Department

Dr. Sandra Ramey, Professor, University of Iowa

Dr. John Violanti, Professor, State University of New York Buffalo

Yost Zakhary, Public Safety Director, City of Woodway, Texas

Panel Two: Officer Safety

Jane Castor, Chief, Tampa (Florida) Police Department

Jerry L. Demings, Sheriff, Orange County (Florida) Sheriff's Office

Dr. Alexander L. Eastman, Lieutenant and Deputy Medical Director, Dallas Police Department

Craig W. Floyd, Chairman and Chief Executive Officer, National Law Enforcement Officers Memorial Fund

Panel Three: Voices from the Field

Dianne Bernhard, Executive Director, Concerns of Police Survivors

Robert Bryant, Chief, Penobscot Nation

Chuck Canterbury, National President, Fraternal Order of Police

William J. Johnson, Executive Director, National Association of Police Organizations

Jonathan Thompson, Executive Director, National Sheriffs' Association

Panel Four: Labor/Management Relations

Dr. Chuck Wexler, Executive Director, Police Executive Research Forum

Karen Freeman-Wilson, Mayor, Gary, Indiana

Mark Magaw, Chief, Prince George's County (Maryland) Police Department

Jim Pasco, Executive Director, Fraternal Order of Police

Dustin Smith, President, Sacramento (California) Police Officers Association

Listening Session 7: Future of Community Policing

Washington, DC, February 24, 2015

Panel: Future of Community Policing

Dr. Phillip Goff, Professor, University of California, Los Angeles

Jim McDonnell, Sheriff, Los Angeles County Sheriff's Department

Dr. Daniel Nagin, Professor, Carnegie Mellon University

Dr. Lawrence Sherman, Professor, University of Cambridge, U.K.

Jeremy Travis, President, John Jay College of Criminal Justice, City University of New York

Appendix B. Individuals & Organizations That Submitted Written Testimony

In addition to receiving testimony from those individuals that appeared as witnesses during public listening sessions, the President's Task Force on 21st Century Policing accepted written testimony from any individual or organization to ensure that its information gathering efforts included as many people and perspectives as possible. The task force thanks the individuals and organizations who submitted written testimony for their time and expertise.

This list reflects organizational affiliation at the time of testimony submission and may not represent submitters' current positions.

Individuals

Robert Abraham, Chair, Gang Resistance Education & Training (GREAT) National Policy Board

Phillip Agnew, Executive Director, Dream Defenders

Kilolo Ajanaku, National Executive Director, World Conference of Mayors' Dr. Martin Luther King, Jr. American Dream Initiative

Barbara Attard, Past President, National Association for Civilian Oversight of Law Enforcement

Paul Babeu, Vice President, Arizona Sheriffs Association

Monifa Bandele, Communities United for Police Reform

Dante Barry, Executive Director, Million Hoodies

Michael Bell, Lt. Colonel (retired), United States Air Force

Michael Berkow, Chief, Savannah (Georgia) Police Department

Greg Berman and **Emily Gold LaGratta**, Center for Court Innovation

Angela Glover Blackwell, Founder and CEO, PolicyLink

Mark Bowman, Assistant Professor of Justice Studies, Methodist University

Eli Briggs, Director of Government Affairs, National Association of County and City Health Officials (NACCHO)

Cherie Brown, Executive Director, National Coalition Building Institute

Steven Brown, Journalist / Public Relations Consultant

Chris Calabrese, Senior Policy Director, Center for Democracy and Technology—with **Jake Laperruque**, Fellow on Privacy, Surveillance, and Security

Melanie Campbell, President and CEO, National Coalition on Black Civic Participation

Mo Canady, Executive Director, National Association of School Resource Officers (NASRO)

Hugh Carter Donahue, Adjunct Professor, Department of History, Rowan University

Anthony Chapa, President, Hispanic American Police Command Officers Association

Lorig Charkoudian, Executive Director, Community Mediation Maryland

Ralph Clark, President and CEO, SST Inc.

Faye Coffield

The Hon. LaDoris Cordell, Office of the Independent Police Auditor, San Jose, California

Jill Corson Lake, Director of Global Advising, Parsons The New School for Design

David Couper, Chief of Police (retired), Minneapolis Police Department

Madeline deLone, Executive Director, The Innocence Project—with Marvin Anderson, Board Member

Jimmie Dotson, Police Chief (retired), Houston Independent School District / GeoDD GeoPolicing Team

Ronnie Dunn, Professor, Cleveland State University

Lauren-Brooke Eisen and Nicole Fortier – Counsel, Justice Program, Brennan Center for Justice at NYU School of Law

Christian Ellis, CEO, Alternative Ballistics

Jeffrey Fagan, Professor of Law, Columbia Law School

Mai Fernandez, Executive Director, National Center for Victims of Crime

Johnny Ford, Founder, Alabama Conference of Black Mayors and Mayor, Tuskegee, Alabama

Lisa Foster, Director, Access to Justice Initiative, U.S. Department of Justice

Neill Franklin, Executive Director, Law Enforcement Against Prohibition

S. Gabrielle Frey, Interim Executive Director, National Association of Community Mediation

Lorie Fridell, Associate Professor of Criminology, University of South Florida

Ethan Garcia, Youth Specialist, Identity Inc.

Michael Gennaco, Principal, OIR Group

Al Gerhardstein, Civil Rights Attorney

James Gierach, Executive Board Vice Chairman, Law Enforcement Against Prohibition

Fred Ginyard, Organizing Director, Fabulous Independent Educated Radical for Community Empowerment (FIERCE)

Mark Gissiner, Past President, International Association for Civilian Oversight of Law Enforcement

Becca Gomby, SDR Academy

Rev. Aaron Graham, Lead Pastor, The District Church

Fatima Graves, Vice President, National Women's Law Center—with Lara S. Kaufmann, Senior Counsel and Director of Education Policy for At-Risk Students

Virgil Green, Chairman, Future America National Crime Solution Commission

Sheldon Greenberg, Professor, School of Education, Division of Public Safety Leadership, The Johns Hopkins University

Robert Haas, Police Commissioner, Cambridge (Massachusetts) Police Department

W. Craig Hartley, Executive Director, CALEA

Steven Hawkins, Executive Director, Amnesty International USA

Louis Hayes, The Virtus Group, Inc.

Wade Henderson, President and CEO, The Leadership Conference on Civil and Human Rights—with Nancy Zirkin, Executive Vice President

Maulin Chris Herring, Trainer/Consultant, Public Safety

Sandy Holman, Director, The Culture CO-OP

Zachary Horn and Kent Halverson, Aptima, Inc.—with Rebecca Damari and Aubrey Logan-Terry, Georgetown University

Tanya Clay House, Director of Public Policy, Lawyers' Committee for Civil Rights Under Law

Melanie Jeffers

Megan Johnston, Executive Director, Northern Virginia Mediation Service

Nola Joyce, Deputy Commissioner, Philadelphia Police Department

Keith Kauffman, Captain, Hawthorne (California) Police Department

Gwendolyn Puryear Keita, Executive Director, American Psychological Association, Public Interest Directorate

Stanley Knee, Chief, Austin (Texas) Police Department

Laura Kunard, Senior Research Scientist, CNA Corporation

David Kurz, Chief, Durham (New Hampshire) Police Department

Deborah Lauter, Director of Civil Rights, Anti-Defamation League—with Michael Lieberman, Washington Counsel

Cynthia Lum and Christopher Koper, George Mason University, Center for Evidence-Based Crime Policy

Bruce Lumpkins

Edward Maguire, Professor of Justice, Law & Criminology, American University

Baron Marquis

Travis Martinez, Lieutenant, Redlands (California) Police Department

Mike Masterson, Chief, Boise (Idaho) Police Department

Andrew Mazzara, Executive Director, International Law Enforcement Forum—with Colin Burrows QMP (U.K.), ILEF Advisory Board Chair

R. Paul McCauley, Past President, Academy of Criminal Justice Sciences

V. Michael McKenzie

Harvey McMurray, Chair, Department of Criminal Justice, North Carolina Central University

Pamela Meanes, President, National Bar Association

Doug Mellis, President, Massachusetts Chiefs of Police Association—with Brian Kyes, President, Massachusetts Major City Chiefs Association

Seth Miller, President, The Innocence Network

Charlene Moe, Program Coordinator, Center for Public Safety and Justice, Institute of Government and Public Affairs, University of Illinois

Marc Morial, CEO, National Urban League

Richard Myers, Chief, Newport News (Virginia) Police Department

Toye Nash, Sergeant, Phoenix Police Department

Rebecca Neri and Anthony Berryman – UCLA Improvement by Design Research Group

Chuck Noerenberg, President, National Alliance for Drug Endangered Children

Newell Normand, Sheriff, Jefferson Parish (Louisiana) Sherriff's Office—submitted with Adrian Garcia, Sheriff, Harris County (Texas) Sheriff's Office; David Mahoney, Sheriff, Dane County (Wisconsin) Sheriff's Office; Anthony Normore, Ph.D., Criminal Justice Commission for Credible Leadership Development; and Mitch Javidi, Ph.D., International Academy of Public Safety

Gbadegesin Olubukola, St. Louis University

Patrice O'Neill, CEO/Executive Producer, Not In Our Town

Jim Palmer, Executive Director, Wisconsin Professional Police Association

Julie Parker, Media Relations Division Director, Prince George's County (Maryland) Police Department

George Patterson, Associate Professor, City University of New York

David Perry, President, International Association of Campus Law Enforcement Administrators (IACLEA)

Megan Price, Director, Insight Conflict Resolution Program, School for Conflict Analysis and Resolution, George Mason University

Sue Quinn, Past President, National Association for Civilian Oversight of Law Enforcement

Tess Raser, Teacher, Brooklyn, New York

Darakshan Raja, Program Manager, Washington Peace Center

Sir Desmond Rea and Robin Masefield, Northern Ireland Policing Board

Nuno Rocha

Edwin Roessler, Jr., Chief, Fairfax County (Virginia) Police Department

Jeffrey Rojek, University of Texas at El Paso

Iris Roley, Black United Front of Cincinnati

Julia Ryan, Community Safety Initiative Director, LISC

Robert Samuels, Former Acting Director, DOJ Executive Office for Weed and Seed

Kami Chavis Simmons, Professor of Law and Director of the Criminal Justice Program, Wake Forest University School of Law

Russell Skiba, Professor and Director, Equity Project at Indiana University

Ronald Sloan, President, Association of State Criminal Investigative Agencies

Samuel Somers, Jr., Chief, Sacramento Police Department

Don Tijerina, President, Hispanic American Police Command Officers Association

Nicholas Turner, President and Director, Vera Institute of Justice

James Unnever, Professor of Criminology, University of South Florida

Javier Valdes, Executive Director, Make the Road New York

Kim Vansell, Director, National Center for Campus Public Safety

Nina Vinik, Program Director, Gun Violence Prevention, The Joyce Foundation

Vincent Warren, Executive Director, Center for Constitutional Rights

Barbara Weinstein, Associate Director, Religious Action Center of Reform Judaism

Jenny Yang, Chair, U.S. Equal Employment Opportunity Commission

Organizations

American Friends Service Committee

American Society of Criminology, Division of Policing, Ad Hoc Committee to the President's Task Force on 21st Century Policing (Anthony Braga, Rod K. Brunson, Gary Cordner, Lorie Fridell, Matthew Hickman, Cynthia Lum, Stephen D. Mastrofski, Jack McDevitt, Dennis P. Rosenbaum, Wesley G. Skogan, and William Terrill)

Center for Popular Democracy

Civil Rights Coalition on Police Reform

CNA Corporation (George Fachner, Michael D. White, James R. Coldren, Jr., and James K. Stewart)

Color of Change

Dignity in Schools Campaign

Ethics Bureau at Yale (Lawrence Fox, Supervising Lawyer)

Evangelical Lutheran Church in America

International Association for Human Values (IAHV) / Works of Wonder International

John F. Kennedy School of Government

Local Initiatives Support Corporation (LISC)

Major County Sheriffs' Association

National Action Network (NAN)

National Association for Civilian Oversight of Law Enforcement

National Association of Counties

National Association of Police Organizations

National Association of Women Law Enforcement Executives

National Collaborative for Health Equity, Dellums Commission

National Fraternal Order of Police

National Organization of Black Law Enforcement Executives (NOBLE)

National Sheriffs' Association

PICO National Network

Public Science Project

Santa Fe College and the Santa Fe Police Department, Gainesville, Florida

Streetwise & Safe

Team Kids

"Think Tank Johnny"

Appendix C. Executive Order 13684 of December 18, 2014

By the authority vested in me as President by the Constitution and the laws of the United States of America, and in order to identify the best means to provide an effective partnership between law enforcement and local communities that reduces crime and increases trust, it is hereby ordered as follows:

Section 1. *Establishment.* There is established a President's Task Force on 21st Century Policing (Task Force).

Sec. 2. *Membership.* (a) The Task Force shall be composed of not more than eleven members appointed by the President. The members shall include distinguished individuals with relevant experience or subject-matter expertise in law enforcement, civil rights, and civil liberties.

(b) The President shall designate two members of the Task Force to serve as Co-Chairs.

Sec. 3. *Mission.* (a) The Task Force shall, consistent with applicable law, identify best practices and otherwisemake recommendations to the President on how policing practices can promote effective crime reduction while building public trust.

(b) The Task Force shall be solely advisory and shall submit a report to the President by March 2, 2015.

Sec. 4. *Administration.* (a) The Task Force shall hold public meetings and engage with Federal, State, tribal, and local officials, technical advisors, and nongovernmental organizations, among others, as necessary to carry out its mission.

(b) The Director of the Office of Community Oriented Policing Services shall serve as Executive Director of the Task Force and shall, as directed by the Co-Chairs, convene regular meetings of the Task Force and supervise its work.

(c) In carrying out its mission, the Task Force shall be informed by, and shall strive to avoid duplicating, the efforts of other governmental entities.

(d) The Department of Justice shall provide administrative services, funds, facilities, staff, equipment, and other support services as may be necessary for the Task Force to carry out its mission to the extent permitted by law and subject to the availability of appropriations.

(e) Members of the Task Force shall serve without any additional compensation for their work on the Task Force, but shall be allowed travel expenses, including per diem, to the extent permitted by law for persons serving intermittently in the Government service (5 U.S.C.5701-5707).

Sec. 5. *Termination.* The Task Force shall terminate 30 days after the President requests a final report from the Task Force.

Sec. 6. *General Provisions.* (a) Nothing in this order shall be construed to impair or otherwise affect:

(i) the authority granted by law to a department, agency, or the head thereof; or

(ii) the functions of the Director of the Office of Management and Budget relating to budgetary, administrative, or legislative proposals.

(b) This order is not intended to, and does not, create any right or benefit, substantive or procedural, enforceable at law or in equity by any party against the United States, its departments, agencies, or entities, its officers, employees, or agents, or any other person.

(c) Insofar as the Federal Advisory Committee Act, as amended (5 U.S.C. App.) (the "Act") may apply to the Task Force, any functions of the President under the Act, except for those in section 6 of the Act, shall be performed by the Attorney General.

THE WHITE HOUSE,
December 18, 2014.

Appendix D. Task Force Members' Biographies

Co-Chairs

Charles Ramsey

Charles Ramsey is the commissioner of the Philadelphia Police Department (PPD), a position he has held since 2008. Since 2010, he has served as president of the Major Cities Chiefs Association and the Police Executive Research Forum. Commissioner Ramsey began his law enforcement career in 1968 as a cadet with the Chicago Police Department (CPD). Over the next 30 years, he held various positions with the CPD, including commander of the Narcotics Division, deputy chief of the Patrol Division, and deputy superintendent, a role he held from 1994 to 1998. In 1998, he was named chief of the Metropolitan Police Department of the District of Columbia (MPDC), where he served until early 2007. In 2007, Commissioner Ramsey served on the Independent Commission on Security Forces of Iraq, leading a review of the Iraqi Police Force. In addition to his current role at the PPD, he also serves as a member of the Homeland Security Advisory Council. Commissioner Ramsey received a BS and MS from Lewis University.

Laurie Robinson

Laurie Robinson is the Clarence J. Robinson Professor of Criminology, Law and Society at George Mason University, a position she has held since 2012. She served as assistant attorney general for the Office of Justice Programs (OJP) in the U.S. Department of Justice (DOJ) from 2009 to 2012. Prior to that, Ms. Robinson served as the Principal deputy assistant attorney general for OJP and acting assistant attorney general for OJP. Previously, she was a member of the Obama-Biden Transition Team. From 2003 to 2009, Ms. Robinson was the director of the Master of Science Program in Criminology at the University of Pennsylvania. From 1993 to 2000, she served her first term as assistant attorney general for OJP. Before joining DOJ, Ms. Robinson spent over 20 years with the American Bar Association, serving as assistant staff director of the Criminal Justice Section from 1972 to 1979, director of the Criminal Justice Section from 1979 to 1993, and director of the Professional Services Division from 1986 to 1993. She is a senior fellow at the George Mason University Center for Evidence-Based Crime Policy and serves as co-chair of the Research Advisory Committee for the International Association of Chiefs of Police. She also serves on the board of trustees of the Vera Institute of Justice. Ms. Robinson received a BA from Brown University.

Members

Cedric L. Alexander

Cedric L. Alexander is the deputy chief operating officer for Public Safety in DeKalb County, Georgia, a position he has held since late 2013. Dr. Alexander is also the national president of the National Organization of Black Law Enforcement Executives. In 2013, he served as chief of police for the DeKalb County Police Department. Prior to this, Dr. Alexander served as federal security director for the Transportation Security Administration (TSA) at Dallas/Fort Worth International Airport from 2007 to 2013. And from 2006 to 2007, he was deputy commissioner of the New York State Division of Criminal

Justice Services. From 2005 to 2006, Dr. Alexander was chief of the Rochester (New York) Police Department (RPD), where he previously served as deputy chief of police from 2002 to 2005. Before joining RPD, Dr. Alexander was a faculty member in the Department of Psychiatry at the University of Rochester Medical Center from 1998 to 2002. He began his career as a deputy sheriff in Florida from 1977 to 1981, before joining the Miami-Dade Police Department, where he was as an officer and detective from 1981 to 1992. He received a BA and MS from St. Thomas University in Miami, Florida, and a PsyD from Wright State University.

Jose Lopez

Jose Lopez is currently the lead organizer at Make the Road New York (MRNY), a Brooklyn-based non-profit community organization focused on civil rights, education reform, and combating poverty. He became lead organizer of MRNY in 2013. Mr. Lopez began his career in 2000 as youth organizer with Make the Road by Walking, which later merged with the Latin American Integration Center to form MRNY in 2007. He continued to serve as youth organizer with MRNY until 2009 when he became senior organizer. Since 2011, Mr. Lopez has represented MRNY on the steering committee of Communities United for Police Reform, a New York City organization advocating for law enforcement reform. From 2001 to 2004, he was an active contributor to the Radio Rookies Project, an initiative of New York Public Radio. He received a BA from Hofstra University.

Tracey L. Meares

Tracey Meares is the Walton Hale Hamilton Professor of Law at Yale Law School, a position she has held since 2007. From 2009 to 2011, she also served as deputy dean of Yale Law School. Before joining the faculty at Yale, she served as a professor at the University of Chicago Law School from 1995 to 2007. She has served on the Committee on Law and Justice, a National Research Council Standing Committee of the National Academy of Sciences. She was appointed by Attorney General Eric Holder to serve on the inaugural U.S. Department of Justice, Office of Justice Programs Science Advisory Board. She also currently serves on the board of directors of the Joyce Foundation. Ms. Meares began her legal career as a law clerk for Judge Harlington Wood, Jr. of the U.S. Court of Appeals for the Seventh Circuit. She later served as a trial attorney in the Antitrust Division at the U.S. Department of Justice. Ms. Meares received a BS from the University of Illinois and a JD from the University of Chicago Law School.

Brittany N. Packnett

Brittany Packnett is currently executive director of Teach For America in St. Louis, Missouri, a position she has held since 2012. From 2010 to 2012, she was a director on the Government Affairs Team at Teach For America. Ms. Packnett was a legislative assistant for the U.S. House of Representatives from 2009 to 2010. From 2007 to 2009, she was a third grade teacher in Southeast Washington, D.C., as a member of the Teach For America Corps. Ms. Packnett has volunteered as executive director of Dream Girls DMV, a mentoring program for young girls, and was the founding co-chair of The Collective-DC, a regional organization for Teach For America alumni of color. She currently serves on the board of New City School, the COCA (Center of Creative Arts) Associate Board, the Urban League of Metro St. Louis Education Committee, and the John Burroughs School Board Diversity Committee. Ms. Packnett received a BA from Washington University in St. Louis and an MA from American University.

Susan Lee Rahr

Susan Rahr is executive director of the Washington State Criminal Justice Training Commission, a position she has held since 2012. From 2005 to 2012, she served as the first female sheriff in King County, Washington. Ms. Rahr spent over 30 years as a law enforcement officer, beginning as a patrol officer and undercover narcotics officer. While serving with the King County Sheriff's Office, she held various positions including serving as the commander of the Internal Investigations and Gang Units; commander of the Special Investigations Section; and police chief of Shoreline, Washington. Ms. Rahr received a BA from Washington State University. She has served as a member of the National Institute of Justice and Harvard Kennedy School Executive Session on Policing and Public Safety; president of the Washington State Association of Sheriffs and Police Chiefs, and an executive board member of the National Sheriffs' Association.

Constance Rice

Constance Rice is a civil rights attorney and co-director of the Advancement Project, an organization she co-founded in 1999. In 2003, Ms. Rice was selected to lead the Blue Ribbon Rampart Review Panel, which investigated the largest police corruption scandal in Los Angeles Police Department history. In 1991, Ms. Rice joined the NAACP Legal Defense and Educational Fund, and she became co-director of the Los Angeles office in 1996. She was previously an associate at Morrison & Foerster and began her legal career as a law clerk to Judge Damon J. Keith of the U.S. Court of Appeals for the Sixth Circuit. Ms. Rice received a BA from Harvard College and a JD from the New York University School of Law.

Sean Michael Smoot

Sean Smoot is currently director and chief counsel for the Police Benevolent & Protective Association of Illinois (PB&PA) and the Police Benevolent Labor Committee (PBLC), positions he has held since 2000. He began his career with PB&PA and PBLC as a staff attorney in 1995, before becoming chief counsel of both organizations in 1997. Since 2001, Mr. Smoot has served as the treasurer of the National Association of Police Organizations and has served on the Advisory Committee for the National Law Enforcement Officers' Rights Center since 1996. From 2008 to 2009, he was a policy advisor to the Obama-Biden Transition Project on public safety and state and local police issues and was a member of the National Institute of Justice and Harvard Kennedy School of Government Executive Session on Policing and Public Safety from 2008 to 2011. Mr. Smoot served as police commissioner of Leland Grove, Illinois, from 1998 to 2008. He received a BS from Illinois State University and a JD from Southern Illinois University School of Law.

Bryan Stevenson

Bryan Stevenson is founder and executive director of the Equal Justice Initiative (EJI), a private, nonprofit organization headquartered in Montgomery, Alabama. In addition to directing the EJI since 1989, he is a clinical professor at New York University School of Law. He previously has served as a visiting professor of law at the University of Michigan School of Law. Mr. Stevenson has received the American Bar Association's Wisdom Award for public service, the ACLU's National Medal of Liberty, and the MacArthur Foundation "Genius" Award Prize. Mr. Stevenson received a BA from Eastern College (now Eastern University), a JD from Harvard Law School, and an MPP from the John F. Kennedy School of Government at Harvard University.

Roberto Villaseñor

Roberto Villaseñor is chief of police for the Tucson (Arizona) Police Department (TPD), a position he has held since 2009. He joined the TPD in 1980 and has served as officer, sergeant, lieutenant, and captain and as assistant chief from 2000 to 2009. Chief Villaseñor was named Officer of the Year for the TPD in 1996 and has been awarded the TPD Medal of Merit three times. He also received the TPD Medal of Distinguished Service. Chief Villaseñor is the incoming president of the Arizona Association of Chiefs of Police and a board member of the Police Executive Research Forum (PERF). He received a BS from Park University and a MEd from Northern Arizona University.

Appendix E. Recommendations and Actions

0.1 OVERARCHING RECOMMENDATION: The President should support and provide funding for the creation of a National Crime and Justice Task Force to review and evaluate all components of the criminal justice system for the purpose of making recommendations to the country on comprehensive criminal justice reform.

0.2 OVERARCHING RECOMMENDATION: The President should promote programs that take a comprehensive and inclusive look at community based initiatives that address the core issues of poverty, education, health, and safety.

1.1 RECOMMENDATION: Law enforcement culture should embrace a guardian mindset to build public trust and legitimacy. Toward that end, police and sheriffs' departments should adopt procedural justice as the guiding principle for internal and external policies and practices to guide their interactions with the citizens they serve.

1.2 RECOMMENDATION: Law enforcement agencies should acknowledge the role of policing in past and present injustice and discrimination and how it is a hurdle to the promotion of community trust.

> 1.2.1 ACTION ITEM: The U.S. Department of Justice should develop and disseminate case studies that provide examples where past injustices were publically acknowledged by law enforcement agencies in a manner to help build community trust.

1.3 RECOMMENDATION: Law enforcement agencies should establish a culture of transparency and accountability in order to build public trust and legitimacy. This will help ensure decision making is understood and in accord with stated policy.

> 1.3.1 ACTION ITEM: To embrace a culture of transparency, law enforcement agencies should make all department policies available for public review and regularly post on the department's website information about stops, summonses, arrests, reported crime, and other law enforcement data aggregated by demographics.

> 1.3.2 ACTION ITEM: When serious incidents occur, including those involving alleged police misconduct, agencies should communicate with citizens and the media swiftly, openly, and neutrally, respecting areas where the law requires confidentiality.

1.4 RECOMMENDATION: Law enforcement agencies should promote legitimacy internally within the organization by applying the principles of procedural justice.

> 1.4.1 ACTION ITEM: In order to achieve internal legitimacy, law enforcement agencies should involve employees in the process of developing policies and procedures.

> 1.4.2 ACTION ITEM: Law enforcement agency leadership should examine opportunities to incorporate procedural justice into the internal discipline process, placing additional importance on values adherence rather than adherence to rules. Union leadership should be partners in this process.

1.5 RECOMMENDATION: Law enforcement agencies should proactively promote public trust by initiating positive nonenforcement activities to engage communities that typically have high rates of investigative and enforcement involvement with government agencies.

1.5.1 ACTION ITEM: In order to achieve external legitimacy, law enforcement agencies should involve the community in the process of developing and evaluating policies and procedures.

1.5.2 ACTION ITEM: Law enforcement agencies should institute residency incentive programs such as Resident Officer Programs.

1.5.3 ACTION ITEM: Law enforcement agencies should create opportunities in schools and communities for positive, nonenforcement interactions with police. Agencies should also publicize the beneficial outcomes and images of positive, trust-building partnerships and initiatives.

1.5.4 ACTION ITEM: Use of physical control equipment and techniques against vulnerable populations—including children, elderly persons, pregnant women, people with physical and mental disabilities, limited English proficiency, and others—can undermine public trust and should be used as a last resort. Law enforcement agencies should carefully consider and review their policies towards these populations and adopt policies if none are in place.

1.6 RECOMMENDATION: Law enforcement agencies should consider the potential damage to public trust when implementing crime fighting strategies.

1.6.1 ACTION ITEM: Research conducted to evaluate the effectiveness of crime fighting strategies should specifically look at the potential for collateral damage of any given strategy on community trust and legitimacy.

1.7 RECOMMENDATION: Law enforcement agencies should track the level of trust in police by their communities just as they measure changes in crime. Annual community surveys, ideally standardized across jurisdictions and with accepted sampling protocols, can measure how policing in that community affects public trust.

1.7.1 ACTION ITEM: The Federal Government should develop survey tools and instructions for use of such a model to prevent local departments from incurring the expense and to allow for consistency across jurisdictions.

1.8 RECOMMENDATION: Law enforcement agencies should strive to create a workforce that contains a broad range of diversity including race, gender, language, life experience, and cultural background to improve understanding and effectiveness in dealing with all communities.

1.8.1 ACTION ITEM: The Federal Government should create a Law Enforcement Diversity Initiative designed to help communities diversify law enforcement departments to reflect the demographics of the community.

1.8.2 ACTION ITEM: The department overseeing this initiative should help localities learn best practices for recruitment, training, and outreach to improve the diversity as well as the cultural and linguistic responsiveness of law enforcement agencies.

1.8.3 ACTION ITEM: Successful law enforcement agencies should be highlighted and celebrated and those with less diversity should be offered technical assistance to facilitate change.

1.8.4 ACTION ITEM: Discretionary federal funding for law enforcement programs could be influenced by that department's efforts to improve their diversity and cultural and linguistic responsiveness.

1.8.5 ACTION ITEM: Law enforcement agencies should be encouraged to explore more flexible staffing models.

1.9 RECOMMENDATION: Law enforcement agencies should build relationships based on trust with immigrant communities. This is central to overall public safety.

1.9.1 ACTION ITEM: Decouple federal immigration enforcement from routine local policing for civil enforcement and nonserious crime.

1.9.2 ACTION ITEM: Law enforcement agencies should ensure reasonable and equitable language access for all persons who have encounters with police or who enter the criminal justice system.

1.9.3 ACTION ITEM: The U.S. Department of Justice should remove civil immigration information from the FBI's National Crime Information Center database.

2.1 RECOMMENDATION: Law enforcement agencies should collaborate with community members to develop policies and strategies in communities and neighborhoods disproportionately affected by crime for deploying resources that aim to reduce crime by improving relationships, greater community engagement, and cooperation.

2.1.1 ACTION ITEM: The Federal Government should incentivize this collaboration through a variety of programs that focus on public health, education, mental health, and other programs not traditionally part of the criminal justice system.

2.2 RECOMMENDATION: Law enforcement agencies should have comprehensive policies on the use of force that include training, investigations, prosecutions, data collection, and information sharing. These policies must be clear, concise, and openly available for public inspection.

2.2.1 ACTION ITEM: Law enforcement agency policies for training on use of force should emphasize de-escalation and alternatives to arrest or summons in situations where appropriate.

2.2.2 ACTION ITEM: These policies should also mandate external and independent criminal investigations in cases of police use of force resulting in death, officer-involved shootings resulting in injury or death, or in-custody deaths.

2.2.3 ACTION ITEM: The task force encourages policies that mandate the use of external and independent prosecutors in cases of police use of force resulting in death, officer-involved shootings resulting in injury or death, or in-custody deaths.

2.2.4 ACTION ITEM: Policies on use of force should also require agencies to collect, maintain, and report data to the Federal Government on all officer-involved shootings, whether fatal or nonfatal, as well as any in-custody death.

2.2.5 ACTION ITEM: Policies on use of force should clearly state what types of information will be released, when, and in what situation, to maintain transparency.

2.2.6 ACTION ITEM: Law enforcement agencies should establish a Serious Incident Review Board comprising sworn staff and community members to review cases involving officer involved shootings and other serious incidents that have the potential to damage community trust or confidence in the agency. The purpose of this board should be to identify any administrative, supervisory, training, tactical, or policy issues that need to be addressed.

2.3 RECOMMENDATION: Law enforcement agencies are encouraged to implement nonpunitive peer review of critical incidents separate from criminal and administrative investigations.

2.4 RECOMMENDATION: Law enforcement agencies are encouraged to adopt identification procedures that implement scientifically supported practices that eliminate or minimize presenter bias or influence.

2.5 RECOMMENDATION: All federal, state, local, and tribal law enforcement agencies should report and make available to the public census data regarding the composition of their departments including race, gender, age, and other relevant demographic data.

2.5.1 ACTION ITEM: The Bureau of Justice Statistics should add additional demographic questions to the Law Enforcement Management and Administrative Statistics (LEMAS) survey in order to meet the intent of this recommendation.

2.6 RECOMMENDATION: Law enforcement agencies should be encouraged to collect, maintain, and analyze demographic data on all detentions (stops, frisks, searches, summons, and arrests). This data should be disaggregated by school and non-school contacts.

2.6.1 ACTION ITEM: The Federal Government could further incentivize universities and other organizations to partner with police departments to collect data and develop knowledge about analysis and benchmarks as well as to develop tools and templates that help departments manage data collection and analysis.

2.7 RECOMMENDATION: Law enforcement agencies should create policies and procedures for policing mass demonstrations that employ a continuum of managed tactical resources that are designed to minimize the appearance of a military operation and avoid using provocative tactics and equipment that undermine civilian trust.

2.7.1. ACTION ITEM: Law enforcement agency policies should address procedures for implementing a layered response to mass demonstrations that prioritize de-escalation and a guardian mindset.

2.7.2 ACTION ITEM: The Federal Government should create a mechanism for investigating complaints and issuing sanctions regarding the inappropriate use of equipment and tactics during mass demonstrations.

2.8 RECOMMENDATION: Some form of civilian oversight of law enforcement is important in order to strengthen trust with the community. Every community should define the appropriate form and structure of civilian oversight to meet the needs of that community.

2.8.1 ACTION ITEM: The U.S. Department of Justice, through its research arm, the National Institute of Justice (NIJ), should expand its research agenda to include civilian oversight.

2.8.2 ACTION ITEM: The U.S. Department of Justice's Office of Community Oriented Policing Services (COPS Office) should provide technical assistance and collect best practices from existing civilian oversight efforts and be prepared to help cities create this structure, potentially with some matching grants and funding.

2.9 RECOMMENDATION: Law enforcement agencies and municipalities should refrain from practices requiring officers to issue a predetermined number of tickets, citations, arrests, or summonses, or to initiate investigative contacts with citizens for reasons not directly related to improving public safety, such as generating revenue.

2.10 RECOMMENDATION: Law enforcement officers should be required to seek consent before a search and explain that a person has the right to refuse consent when there is no warrant or probable cause. Furthermore, officers should ideally obtain written acknowledgement that they have sought consent to a search in these circumstances.

2.12 RECOMMENDATION: Law enforcement agencies should adopt and enforce policies prohibiting profiling and discrimination based on race, ethnicity, national origin, age, gender, gender identity/expression, sexual orientation, immigration status, disability, housing status, occupation, and/or language fluency.

2.12.1 ACTION ITEM: The Bureau of Justice Statistics should add questions concerning sexual harassment of and misconduct toward LGBTQ and gender-nonconforming people by law enforcement officers to the Police Public Contact Survey.

2.12.2 ACTION ITEM: The Centers for Disease Control should add questions concerning sexual harassment of and misconduct toward LGBTQ and gender-nonconforming people by law enforcement officers to the National Intimate Partner and Sexual Violence Survey.

2.12.3 ACTION ITEM: The U.S. Department of Justice should promote and disseminate guidance to federal, state, and local law enforcement agencies on documenting, preventing, and addressing sexual harassment and misconduct by local law enforcement agents, consistent with the recommendations of the International Association of Chiefs of Police.

2.13 RECOMMENDATION: The U.S. Department of Justice, through the Office of Community Oriented Policing Services and Office of Justice Programs, should provide technical assistance and incentive funding to jurisdictions with small police agencies that take steps towards shared services, regional training, and consolidation.

2.14 RECOMMENDATION: The U.S. Department of Justice, through the Office of Community Oriented Policing Services, should partner with the International Association of Directors of Law Enforcement Standards and Training (IADLEST) to expand its National Decertification Index to serve as the National Register of Decertified Officers with the goal of covering all agencies within the United States and its territories.

2.15 RECOMMENDATION: Law enforcement agencies should adopt policies requiring officers to provide their names to individuals they have stopped, along with the reason for the stop, the reason for a search if one is conducted, and a card with information on how to reach the civilian complaint review board.

3.1 RECOMMENDATION: The U.S. Department of Justice, in consultation with the law enforcement field, should broaden the efforts of the National Institute of Justice to establish national standards for the research and development of new technology. These standards should also address compatibility and interoperability needs both within law enforcement agencies and across agencies and jurisdictions and maintain civil and human rights protections.

> 3.1.1 ACTION ITEM: The Federal Government should support the development and delivery of training to help law enforcement agencies learn, acquire, and implement technology tools and tactics that are consistent with the best practices of 21st century policing.

> 3.1.2 ACTION ITEM: As part of national standards, the issue of technology's impact on privacy concerns should be addressed in accordance with protections provided by constitutional law.

> 3.1.3 ACTION ITEM: Law enforcement agencies should deploy smart technology that is designed to prevent the tampering with or manipulating of evidence in violation of policy.

3.2 RECOMMENDATION: The implementation of appropriate technology by law enforcement agencies should be designed considering local needs and aligned with national standards.

> 3.2.1 ACTION ITEM: Law enforcement agencies should encourage public engagement and collaboration, including the use of community advisory bodies, when developing a policy for the use of a new technology.

> 3.2.2 ACTION ITEM: Law enforcement agencies should include an evaluation or assessment process to gauge the effectiveness of any new technology, soliciting input from all levels of the agency, from line officer to leadership, as well as assessment from members of the community.

> 3.2.3. ACTION ITEM: Law enforcement agencies should adopt the use of new technologies that will help them better serve people with special needs or disabilities.

3.3 RECOMMENDATION: The U.S. Department of Justice should develop best practices that can be adopted by state legislative bodies to govern the acquisition, use, retention, and dissemination of auditory, visual, and biometric data by law enforcement.

> 3.3.1 ACTION ITEM: As part of the process for developing best practices, the U.S. Department of Justice should consult with civil rights and civil liberties organizations, as well as law enforcement research groups and other experts, concerning the constitutional issues that can arise as a result of the use of new technologies.

> 3.3.2 ACTION ITEM: The U.S. Department of Justice should create toolkits for the most effective and constitutional use of multiple forms of innovative technology that will provide state, local, and tribal law enforcement agencies with a one-stop clearinghouse of information and resources.

> 3.3.3. ACTION ITEM: Law enforcement agencies should review and consider the Bureau of Justice Assistance's (BJA) Body Worn Camera Toolkit to assist in implementing BWCs.

3.4 RECOMMENDATION: Federal, state, local, and tribal legislative bodies should be encouraged to update public record laws.

3.5 RECOMMENDATION: Law enforcement agencies should adopt model policies and best practices for technology-based community engagement that increases community trust and access.

3.6 RECOMMENDATION: The Federal Government should support the development of new "less than lethal" technology to help control combative suspects.

> 3.6.1 ACTION ITEM: Relevant federal agencies, including the U.S. Departments of Defense and Justice, should expand their efforts to study the development and use of new less than lethal technologies and evaluate their impact on public safety, reducing lethal violence against citizens, Constitutionality, and officer safety.

3.7 RECOMMENDATION: The Federal Government should make the development and building of segregated radio spectrum and increased bandwidth by FirstNet for exclusive use by local, state, tribal, and federal public safety agencies a top priority.

4.1 RECOMMENDATION: Law enforcement agencies should develop and adopt policies and strategies that reinforce the importance of community engagement in managing public safety.

> 4.1.1 ACTION ITEM: Law enforcement agencies should consider adopting preferences for seeking "least harm" resolutions, such as diversion programs or warnings and citations in lieu of arrest for minor infractions.

4.2 RECOMMENDATION: Community policing should be infused throughout the culture and organizational structure of law enforcement agencies.

4.2.1 ACTION ITEM: Law enforcement agencies should evaluate officers on their efforts to engage members of the community and the partnerships they build. Making this part of the performance evaluation process places an increased value on developing partnerships.

4.2.2 ACTION ITEM: Law enforcement agencies should evaluate their patrol deployment practices to allow sufficient time for patrol officers to participate in problem solving and community engagement activities.

4.2.3 ACTION ITEM: The U.S. Department of Justice and other public and private entities should support research into the factors that have led to dramatic successes in crime reduction in some communities through the infusion of non-discriminatory policing and to determine replicable factors that could be used to guide law enforcement agencies in other communities.

4.3 RECOMMENDATION: Law enforcement agencies should engage in multidisciplinary, community team approaches for planning, implementing, and responding to crisis situations with complex causal factors.

4.3.1 ACTION ITEM: The U.S. Department of Justice should collaborate with others to develop and disseminate baseline models of this crisis intervention team approach that can be adapted to local contexts.

4.3.3 ACTION ITEM: Communities should look to involve peer support counselors as part of multidisciplinary teams when appropriate. Persons who have experienced the same trauma can provide both insight to the first responders and immediate support to individuals in crisis.

4.3.4 ACTION ITEM: Communities should be encouraged to evaluate the efficacy of these crisis intervention team approaches and hold agency leaders accountable for outcomes.

4.4 RECOMMENDATION: Communities should support a culture and practice of policing that reflects the values of protection and promotion of the dignity of all, especially the most vulnerable.

4.4.1 ACTION ITEM: Because offensive or harsh language can escalate a minor situation, law enforcement agencies should underscore the importance of language used and adopt policies directing officers to speak to individuals with respect.

4.4.1 ACTION ITEM: Law enforcement agencies should develop programs that create opportunities for patrol officers to regularly interact with neighborhood residents, faith leaders, and business leaders.

4.5 RECOMMENDATION: Community policing emphasizes working with neighborhood residents to co-produce public safety. Law enforcement agencies should work with community residents to identify problems and collaborate on implementing solutions that produce meaningful results for the community.

4.5.1 ACTION ITEM: Law enforcement agencies should schedule regular forums and meetings where all community members can interact with police and help influence programs and policy.

4.5.2 Action Item: Law enforcement agencies should engage youth and communities in joint training with law enforcement, citizen academies, ride-alongs, problem solving teams, community action teams, and quality of life teams.

4.5.3. Action Item: Law enforcement agencies should establish formal community/citizen advisory committees to assist in developing crime prevention strategies and agency policies as well as provide input on policing issues.

4.5.4 Action Item: Law enforcement agencies should adopt community policing strategies that support and work in concert with economic development efforts within communities.

4.6 Recommendation: Communities should adopt policies and programs that address the needs of children and youth most at risk for crime or violence and reduce aggressive law enforcement tactics that stigmatize youth and marginalize their participation in schools and communities.

4.6.1 Action Item: Education and criminal justice agencies at all levels of government should work together to reform policies and procedures that push children into the juvenile justice system.

4.6.2 Action Item: In order to keep youth in school and to keep them from criminal and violent behavior, law enforcement agencies should work with schools to encourage the creation of alternatives to student suspensions and expulsion through restorative justice, diversion, counseling, and family interventions.

4.6.3 Action Item: Law enforcement agencies should work with schools to encourage the use of alternative strategies that involve youth in decision making, such as restorative justice, youth courts, and peer interventions.

4.6.4 Action Item: Law enforcement agencies should work with schools to adopt an instructional approach to discipline that uses interventions or disciplinary consequences to help students develop new behavior skills and positive strategies to avoid conflict, redirect energy, and refocus on learning.

4.6.5 Action Item: Law enforcement agencies should work with schools to develop and monitor school discipline policies with input and collaboration from school personnel, students, families, and community members. These policies should prohibit the use of corporal punishment and electronic control devices.

4.6.6 Action Item: Law enforcement agencies should work with schools to create a continuum of developmentally appropriate and proportional consequences for addressing ongoing and escalating student misbehavior after all appropriate interventions have been attempted.

4.6.7 Action Item: Law enforcement agencies should work with communities to play a role in programs and procedures to reintegrate juveniles back into their communities as they leave the juvenile justice system.

4.6.8 ACTION ITEM: Law enforcement agencies and schools should establish memoranda of agreement for the placement of School Resource Officers that limit police involvement in student discipline.

4.6.9 ACTION ITEM: The Federal Government should assess and evaluate zero tolerance strategies and examine the role of reasonable discretion when dealing with adolescents in consideration of their stages of maturation or development.

4.7 RECOMMENDATION: Communities need to affirm and recognize the voices of youth in community decision making, facilitate youth-led research and problem solving, and develop and fund youth leadership training and life skills through positive youth/police collaboration and interactions.

4.7.1 ACTION ITEM: Communities and law enforcement agencies should restore and build trust between youth and police by creating programs and projects for positive, consistent, and persistent interaction between youth and police.

4.7.2 ACTION ITEM: Communities should develop community- and school-based evidence-based programs that mitigate punitive and authoritarian solutions to teen problems.

5.1 RECOMMENDATION: The Federal Government should support the development of partnerships with training facilities across the country to promote consistent standards for high quality training and establish training innovation hubs.

5.1.1 ACTION ITEM: The training innovation hubs should develop replicable model programs that use adult-based learning and scenario based training in a training environment modeled less like boot camp. Through these programs the hubs would influence nationwide curricula, as well as instructional methodology.

5.1.2 ACTION ITEM: The training innovation hubs should establish partnerships with academic institutions to develop rigorous training practices, evaluation, and the development of curricula based on evidence-based practices.

5.1.3 ACTION ITEM: The Department of Justice should build a stronger relationship with the International Association of Directors of Law Enforcement (IADLEST) in order to leverage their network with state boards and commissions of Peace Officer Standards and Training (POST).

5.2 RECOMMENDATION: Law enforcement agencies should engage community members in the training process.

5.2.1 ACTION ITEM: The U.S. Department of Justice should conduct research to develop and disseminate a toolkit on how law enforcement agencies and training programs can integrate community members into this training process.

5.3 RECOMMENDATION: Law enforcement agencies should provide leadership training to all personnel throughout their careers.

>   5.3.1 ACTION ITEM: Recognizing that strong, capable leadership is required to create cultural transformation, the U.S. Department of Justice should invest in developing learning goals and model curricula/training for each level of leadership.

>   5.3.2 ACTION ITEM: The Federal Government should encourage and support partnerships between law enforcement and academic institutions to support a culture that values ongoing education and the integration of current research into the development of training, policies, and practices.

>   5.3.3 ACTION ITEM: The U.S. Department of Justice should support and encourage cross-discipline leadership training.

5.4 RECOMMENDATION: The U.S. Department of Justice should develop, in partnership with institutions of higher education, a national postgraduate institute of policing for senior executives with a standardized curriculum preparing them to lead agencies in the 21st century.

5.5 RECOMMENDATION: The U.S. Department of Justice should instruct the Federal Bureau of Investigation to modify the curriculum of the National Academy at Quantico to include prominent coverage of the topical areas addressed in this report. In addition, the COPS Office and the Office of Justice Programs should work with law enforcement professional organizations to encourage modification of their curricula in a similar fashion.

5.6 RECOMMENDATION: POSTs should make Crisis Intervention Training (CIT) a part of both basic recruit and in-service officer training.

>   5.6.1 ACTION ITEM: Because of the importance of this issue, Congress should appropriate funds to help support law enforcement crisis intervention training.

5.7 RECOMMENDATION: POSTs should ensure that basic officer training includes lessons to improve social interaction as well as tactical skills.

5.8 RECOMMENDATION: POSTs should ensure that basic recruit and in-service officer training include curriculum on the disease of addiction.

5.9 RECOMMENDATION: POSTs should ensure both basic recruit and in-service training incorporates content around recognizing and confronting implicit bias and cultural responsiveness.

>   5.9.1 ACTION ITEM: Law enforcement agencies should implement ongoing, top down training for all officers in cultural diversity and related topics that can build trust and legitimacy in diverse communities. This should be accomplished with the assistance of advocacy groups that represent the viewpoints of communities that have traditionally had adversarial relationships with law enforcement.

5.9.2 ACTION ITEM: Law enforcement agencies should implement training for officers that covers policies for interactions with the LGBTQ population, including issues such as determining gender identity for arrest placement, the Muslim, Arab, and South Asian communities, and immigrant or non-English speaking groups, as well as reinforcing policies for the prevention of sexual misconduct and harassment.

5.10 RECOMMENDATION: POSTs should require both basic recruit and in-service training on policing in a democratic society.

5.11 RECOMMENDATION: The Federal Government, as well as state and local agencies, should encourage and incentivize higher education for law enforcement officers.

5.11.1 ACTION ITEM: The Federal Government should create a loan repayment and forgiveness incentive program specifically for policing.

5.12 RECOMMENDATION: The Federal Government should support research into the development of technology that enhances scenario based training, social interaction skills, and enables the dissemination of interactive distance learning for law enforcement.

5.13 RECOMMENDATION: The U.S. Department of Justice should support the development and implementation of improved Field Training Officer programs.

5.13.1 ACTION ITEM: The U.S. Department of Justice should support the development of broad Field Training Program standards and training strategies that address changing police culture and organizational procedural justice issues that agencies can adopt and customize to local needs.

5.13.2 ACTION ITEM: The U.S. Department of Justice should provide funding to incentivize agencies to update their Field Training Programs in accordance with the new standards.

6.1 RECOMMENDATION: The U.S. Department of Justice should enhance and further promote its multi-faceted officer safety and wellness initiative.

6.1.1 ACTION ITEM: Congress should establish and fund a national "Blue Alert" warning system.

6.1.2 ACTION ITEM: The U.S. Department of Justice, in partnership with the U.S. Department of Health and Human Services, should establish a task force to study mental health issues unique to officers and recommend tailored treatments.

6.1.3 ACTION ITEM: The Federal Government should support the continuing research into the efficacy of an annual mental health check for officers, as well as fitness, resilience, and nutrition.

6.1.4. ACTION ITEM: Pension plans should recognize fitness for duty examinations as definitive evidence of valid duty or non-duty related disability.

6.1.5 ACTION ITEM: Public Safety Officer Benefits (PSOB) should be provided to survivors of officers killed while working, regardless of whether the officer used safety equipment (seatbelt or anti-ballistic vest) or if officer death was the result of suicide attributed to a current diagnosis of duty-related mental illness, including but not limited to post-traumatic stress disorder (PTSD).

6.2 RECOMMENDATION: Law enforcement agencies should promote safety and wellness at every level of the organization.

6.2.1 ACTION ITEM: Though the Federal Government can support many of the programs and best practices identified by the U.S. Department of Justice initiative described in recommendation 6.1, the ultimate responsibility lies with each agency.

6.3 RECOMMENDATION: The U.S. Department of Justice should encourage and assist departments in the implementation of scientifically supported shift lengths by law enforcement.

6.3.1 ACTION ITEM: The U.S. Department of Justice should fund additional research into the efficacy of limiting the total number of hours an officer should work within a 24–48 hour period, including special findings on the maximum number of hours an officer should work in a high risk or high stress environment (e.g., public demonstrations or emergency situations).

6.4 RECOMMENDATION: Every law enforcement officer should be provided with individual tactical first aid kits and training as well as anti-ballistic vests.

6.4.1 ACTION ITEM: Congress should authorize funding for the distribution of law enforcement individual tactical first-aid kits.

6.4.2 ACTION ITEM: Congress should reauthorize and expand the Bulletproof Vest Partnership (BVP) program.

6.5 RECOMMENDATION: The U.S. Department of Justice should expand efforts to collect and analyze data not only on officer deaths but also on injuries and "near misses."

6.6 RECOMMENDATION: Law enforcement agencies should adopt policies that require officers to wear seat belts and bullet-proof vests and provide training to raise awareness of the consequences of failure to do so.

6.7 RECOMMENDATION: Congress should develop and enact peer review error management legislation.

6.8 RECOMMENDATION: The U.S. Department of Transportation should provide technical assistance opportunities for departments to explore the use of vehicles equipped with vehicle collision prevention "smart car" technology that will reduce the number of accidents.

7.1 RECOMMENDATION: The President should direct all federal law enforcement agencies to review the recommendations made by the Task Force on 21st Century Policing and, to the extent practicable, to adopt those that can be implemented at the federal level.

7.2 RECOMMENDATION: The U.S. Department of Justice should explore public-private partnership opportunities, starting by convening a meeting with local, regional, and national foundations to discuss the proposals for reform described in this report and seeking their engagement and support in advancing implementation of these recommendations.

7.3 RECOMMENDATION: The U.S. Department of Justice should charge its Office of Community Oriented Policing Services (COPS Office) with assisting the law enforcement field in addressing current and future challenges.

For recommendation 7.3, the COPS Office should consider taking actions including but not limited to the following:

- Create a National Policing Practices and Accountability Division within the COPS Office.

- Establish national benchmarks and best practices for federal, state, local, and tribal police departments.

- Provide technical assistance and funding to national, state, local, and tribal accreditation bodies that evaluate policing practices.

- Recommend additional benchmarks and best practices for state training and standards boards.

- Provide technical assistance and funding to state training boards to help them meet national benchmarks and best practices in training methodologies and content.

- Prioritize grant funding to departments meeting benchmarks.

- Support departments through an expansion of the COPS Office Collaborative Reform Initiative.

- Collaborate with universities, the Office of Justice Programs and its bureaus (Bureau of Justice Assistance [BJA], Bureau of Justice Statistics [BJS], National Institute of Justice [NIJ], and Office of Juvenile Justice and Delinquency Prevention [OJJDP]), and others to review research and literature in order to inform law enforcement agencies about evidence-based practices and to identify areas of police operations where additional research is needed.

- Collaborate with the BJS to

    - establish a central repository for data concerning police use of force resulting in death, as well as in-custody deaths, and disseminate this data for use by both community and police;

    - provide local agencies with technical assistance and a template to conduct local citizen satisfaction surveys;

- compile annual citizen satisfaction surveys based on the submission of voluntary local surveys, develop a national level survey as well as surveys for use by local agencies and by small geographic units, and develop questions to be added to the National Crime Victimization Survey relating to citizen satisfaction with police agencies and public trust.

- Collaborate with the BJS and others to develop a template of broader indicators of performance for police departments beyond crime rates alone that could comprise a Uniform Justice Report.

- Collaborate with the NIJ and the BJS to publish an annual report on the "State of Policing" in the United States.

- Provide support to national police leadership associations and national rank and file organizations to encourage them to implement task force recommendations.

- Work with the U.S. Department of Homeland Security to ensure that community policing tactics in state, local, and tribal law enforcement agencies are incorporated into their role in homeland security.

www.ingramcontent.com/pod-product-compliance
Lightning Source LLC
Chambersburg PA
CBHW080305290526
45790CB00005B/1938